Mastering Machine Appliqué
Mock Hand Appliqué and Other Techniques

by Harriet Hargrave

C&T PUBLISHING

Coxcomb or Lotus Flower by Mary Devane. Mock Hand appliqué and machine quilting were used to make this lovely old pattern.

Table of Contents

Primitive Appliqué by Bev Tischhauser. Bev made this sampler during her beginning Mock Hand appliqué class with Barb Eikmeier.

Baltimore Blocks. These four Baltimore blocks, made by Cindy Kraft after a workshop with Elly Sienkiewicz, were sewn totally on the machine. All designs are from the *Baltimore Beauties and Beyond* books.

PART TWO

Mock Hand Appliqué

CHAPTER EIGHT

Equipment

Sewing Machine

As for all sewing machine techniques, a zigzag sewing machine, with basic functions and in excellent working order, is necessary to achieve beautiful hand-stitched effects. (The stitches required for the techniques presented in Part Two are the straight blind stitch and the blanket or buttonhole stitch.)

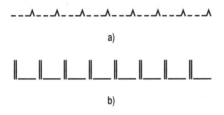

a)

b)

a) Straight blind stitch b) Blanket stitch

In addition, your machine must be fully adjustable for stitch width and length. Check this before you begin your project. Many of the computerized sewing machines being produced today do not allow the operator to override the built-in function of many stitches. The blind stitch is pre-programmed on these machines to go to only number two width (twice as wide as needed), and nothing can be done to overcome this.

If you plan to purchase a machine, consider the types of work you expect to do. If shopping for a computerized machine, look for one that has stepping motors in the stitch width, which allow the needle to be set at *any* stitch width you desire, from "0" to the widest stitch available.

If you have a mechanical machine, check that you have fully adjustable stitch width. Many lower-line machines have only three stitch widths available—narrow, medium, and wide. Another problem is when the stitch selector dial is also the stitch width regulator: when the stitch is selected, the width is also automatically set. If this is the case, the techniques in this book cannot be accomplished successfully.

Adjustable needle position is another helpful feature when working with these stitches. You might find that if your needle is off-center, the toes of the presser foot can be positioned so that guiding is easier on some shapes and projects.

The work surface around your machine is also important. A flat surface at the same level as the needle plate of the machine makes manipulation of the appliqué pieces easier. Otherwise, the fabric is constantly falling off the open arm or small machine surface. If your machine has a sewing table that came with it, use it. If not, create one from wood or other material that can be cut in the shape of the open arm, attaching legs to make it the same height as the machine. This will free your hands to manipulate the shapes and sew accurately instead of fighting the fabric as it falls off the edge and gets caught on the machine.

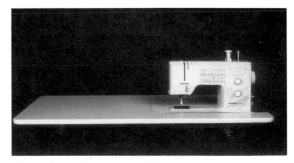

Extension table for machine

Presser Feet

You will be using an open-toe appliqué foot for most of the techniques presented in this unit. When straight stitch techniques are used, you may find it helpful to use an edge stitching foot. This resembles the blind hem foot but does not have the bar that the stitch crosses to add ease in the stitch. The edge stitching foot is used merely for accuracy. Most importantly, your vision should not be hindered by anything in front of the needle when doing the very close work of these techniques; you must be able to see every stitch as it is being made.

a) Bottom of open-toe foot b) Open-toe foot
c) Edge stitching foot

Needles

For the techniques presented here, the use of size 60/8, 65/9 or 70/10 needles is required. These needles are very fine, allowing the stitch holes to become invisible and the tension adjustments to be finer-tuned. If the size 70/10 needle leaves a large hole in the fabric or if the bobbin thread continually peeps up into the hole, change to a smaller needle. If you are using the very small 60/8 or 65/9 and stitches are skipping or the tension is off, try a 70/10. Practice with different needles until a perfect, invisible stitch is achieved.

Remember to change your needles often. They can be the cause of the majority of stitch problems that machines have, but they are often the last item checked. Keep a good supply of needles on hand, and experiment with the threads you are using on each project on samples before starting to stitch. The stitches used in the following techniques cannot be ripped out easily, and poor quality stitching will ruin the finished appearance of your work. For more detailed information on needles, refer to the Satin Stitch unit, Chapter One, page 13.

Iron

You will need a dry iron that you can work with on small pieces. When ironing small seam allowances over an edge of paper, a large iron can burn fingers and cause sloppy edges. A small travel iron with a sharp point (see picture below) is a good choice. Control with the tip of the iron is the key to success here.

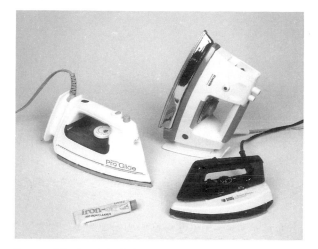

Irons with sharp points

Light Box

A light box is helpful when tracing patterns and placing pieces onto backgrounds. It can be purchased from hobby and art supply stores. Or, make a wood box and put a sheet of glass or Plexiglas on the top, and place a light bulb (or secure small, under-counter fluorescent tubes) in the box. You can also make one at home with your extension table or by simply placing a sheet of glass over the leaf opening of your dining room table and using a bare light bulb in a lamp on the floor underneath the glass.

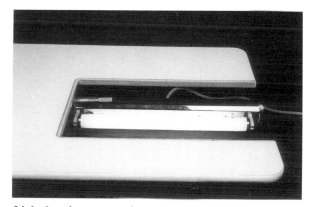

Light box from extension table

The light box enables you to see paper patterns through fabrics, eliminating the step of tracing placement lines onto the fabric itself. Tracing lines tend to be inaccurate, showing outside the edge of the appliqué piece, and hard to remove.

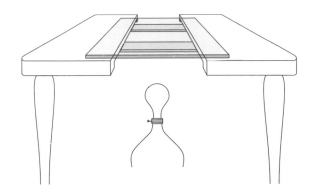

Illustration of dining room table as light box

Photocopy Machine

Having a small, desktop photocopy machine available to you is a real timesaver. The machine must be able to enlarge and reduce, and it must have a manual feeding system as well as a tray feed. You will use it to copy multiple pattern pieces onto freezer paper and to copy directly onto fabric. Details on these ideas are in Chapter Eleven.

Personal photocopy machine

CHAPTER NINE

Supplies

Fabrics

Medium weight 100% cotton fabrics are the easiest to work with when appliquéing. They are very easily turned and manipulated, and they hold a crease well. Polyester blends and other synthetics tend to be more wiry, and it is hard to turn an edge and keep it there. However, the freezer paper techniques presented here will make it easier to work with these more difficult fabrics, if you choose to use them.

Test your fabrics for colorfastness before starting to work with them. Depending on the fabrics' colorfastness to water and detergent, you can prewash them or not. If you do prewash, do not use spray starch or fabric sizing, as these products diminish the adhesion properties of the freezer paper. Some people prefer to work with softer prewashed fabrics; others require the sizing and body of a new fabric. Try working with both, and see which method gives you superior results.

Scissors

Sharp scissors are an important tool in appliqué. You will need a good pair for both paper cutting and for fabric. Paper scissors need to be sharp so that the edges of your paper templates and patterns are smooth and even, not chewed and curled, as often happens with dull or inappropriate scissors. Consider purchasing from an art supply store a pair of paper cutting shears made specifically for cutting layers of paper accurately. I have a pair of Ginghers not only for fabric, but also for paper cutting. My pattern-cutting skills are just as important as the cutting of the fabric, even more so in appliqué.

Ginghers' 5" scissors and 5" tailor-point scissors are excellent for cutting the details of appliqué pieces.

Many people find that the 4" curved blade embroidery scissors are helpful for cutting circles and curved areas. Larger 7" shears are wonderful for cutting long, straight lines or soft, gentle curved areas.

You may also want a tiny pair of very sharp point embroidery scissors for clipping tiny seam allowances. A pair of surgical scissors that have a rounded wedge shaped bottom blade are ideal for cutting away the backs from the appliqués and for trimming. A good collection of scissors in various shapes and sizes will make your cutting work a pleasure, and there is a lot of cutting required in appliqué.

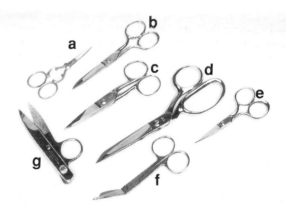

a) Embroidery scissors b) 5" scissors
c) 5" tailor point scissors d) 7" shears
e) Curved blade embroidery scissors
f) Appliqué trim scissors g) Thread clips

Pencils

You will want a supply of pencils with smooth leads (number 2 or 2 ½ works fine). A good quality mechanical pencil is easy to work with and always has a sharp point. Be sure that it is comfortable in your hand, enabling you to trace accurately and easily.

Pins

Look for pins that are very fine in diameter so that the appliqué pieces lie as flat and smooth as possible when pinned in place. Iris™ Swiss Super Fine Pins or sequin pins are excellent for this. Safety pins can also be used. The size "0" or size "1" pins leave very small holes in the fabric and take tight stitches. They also stay in place and don't have exposed points while you are working.

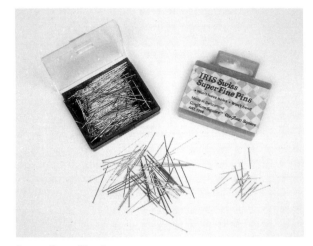

Long fine silk pins

Threads

Only high quality, machine art threads are used in these techniques. Heavier-weight sewing threads make the appliqué appear machine-done.

The bobbin thread will always be 60 weight, 2-ply (60/2) machine embroidery thread. Look for Metrosene/Mettler fine machine embroidery thread. Avoid using basting thread; it is poor quality and is fuzzy enough to distort and add too much bulk to the stitches. Most of the time white will be used, but if you find that your tension cannot be fine-tuned enough to

Various machine embroidery threads

avoid seeing the bobbin thread on the top, use the 60/2 embroidery thread in a color that matches the background fabric color.

For Blanket Stitch appliqué, size 30, 2-ply machine embroidery thread is used in the needle. This is a soft, heavier thread that tends to untwist after the stitch is made, creating the soft, filled-in look of embroidery floss. Thinner embroidery threads do not fill in adequately, and sewing threads are too stiff and coarse.

Size identification on spool

Size .004 invisible monofilament quilting thread is used for the Mock Hand appliqué technique. This is a very soft nylon that allows your machine blind stitch to look just like a hand-stitched edge. It is used only on the top to prevent breakage and jamming. Be very particular when purchasing this thread; if it is too weak or too strong, it will give unsatisfactory results. Buy it on small cones in 1,000- to 1,500-yard quantities. Anything larger than this will age poorly and become brittle before it can be used. Recommended brands are Sew Art International and Wonder Thread from YLI (Yarn Loft International). Look for the label on the bottom of the cone (see above).

When threading the machine with this thread, care must be taken that no drag is put on it. If you have constant tension problems when using the nylon thread, use a cone holder or a small jar that will hold the cone upright off the machine and allow the thread to come off from the top of the cone. Place the thread on the right side and in back of the machine. If no thread guide is available at the spool pin area of the machine, tape a closed safety pin onto the machine at the spool pins so that the thread will track as if it were coming off the pins themselves.

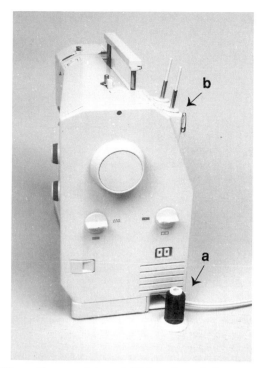

Threading machine a) Nylon thread placement b) Safety pin placement

Fusible products can be timesaving and give a firm edge to work with. Thread Fuse™ is a new fusible thread on the market that can be used only in the bobbin of a machine. It is a core thread that is wrapped with fusible filament. When heated, the thread will fuse to another fabric. It is used for Blanket Stitch appliqué. Fusible hem tape and paper backed fusible webs, such as Wonder-Under and HeatnBond will also be used.

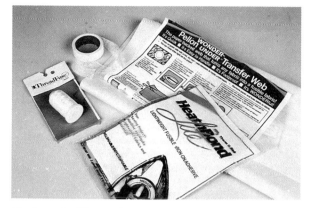

Various fusible products

As you develop your skills in machine appliqué, you will probably be tempted to try various other threads for effect. Rayons and metallics are becoming more popular in machine art work, and the quality of these threads has improved dramatically from what it was a few years ago. Several brands to try include: Sulky® Rayon and Metallic, Madeira® metallic, Natesh® rayon, and Kanagawa metallic.

TIP: When these speciality threads are used, you may find that regular needles do not produce the quality of stitch you desire. The Schmetz blue steel stretch needle in size 75 often helps protect the thread from friction and produces a smoother, finer stitch quality. Experiment with different sizes of needles to obtain the look you desire. A standard size 80/12 or 90/14 might give good results, also.

Freezer Paper

Freezer paper hit the quilting world several years ago and revolutionized the way we prepare appliqué pieces. It comes in two varieties: plain and plastic coated. We will be working with only the plastic coated. You will find this paper at your grocery store with the canning supplies. The brand preferred by most quilters is Reynolds® Freezer Paper Plastic Coated. The plastic coated side adheres to the fabric pieces when a dry iron, at cotton setting, is applied (it is a temporary bonding process). The dull side is used for tracing or drawing. The plastic does not damage the fabric in any way and peels off easily, with no residue, when you are done with it. The paper is fairly durable, easy to fold and cut, transparent for tracing, and gives perfect edges to appliqué pieces.

Specialty threads and needles

Freezer paper and tag board

Tag Board

Tag board is an excellent medium for making templates because it is easily cut and can be used with an iron. It is sold in large sheets in an art supply store. You could also use heavy weight manila filing folders.

Fabric-Basting Glue Sticks
(Aleene's, Dennison, Collins, Dritz, Quilter's Basting GluTube®)

Fresh glue sticks are important when working with the small seam allowances of these techniques. Be sure to work with fabric-basting glue sticks instead of paper glue sticks. A bit of Teflon in fabric glue makes it glide onto the fabric easily. If your glue stick becomes gummy or stringy, replace it with a new one.

TIP: Store glue sticks in the freezer in a sealed recloseable bag. Work with one when it is cold. If it becomes gummy or warm, put it back in the freezer and take out a cold one. The heat of your hand or the humidity in the air can make it very messy to work with. Keep a wet washcloth beside you to keep your fingers clean.

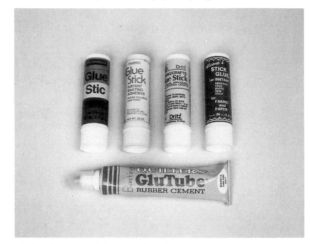

Adhesives used for appliqué

Quilters GluTube is a rubber cement type of glue that temporarily bonds the fabric seam allowances to paper. Using this glue eliminates dampening the fabric to remove paper from the appliqué pieces, but glue is left permanently in the fabric. Read the instructions carefully, and use it in a well ventilated room.

Aqua-Solv and Solvy

These products have been used in machine arts for several years and are now finding their way into quilting. They are water-soluble embroidery facings, made of gelatin, used for placement marking of detail lines for Satin Stitch appliqué and for techniques of Mock Hand appliqué. Easy to use, they dissolve in water by spraying or soaking. Once you have tried them, you will find many other uses for them.

Water-soluable embroidery facings

CHAPTER TEN

Preparation Techniques

The basic preparation of pattern pieces for the machine appliqué techniques presented here are very similar to those used for hand appliqué. In fact, you will find these methods very useful for hand stitching. There are as many ways to prepare for stitching as there are stitchers. I have only presented the ones that seem to be tried-and-true in my classrooms. Don't hesitate to adapt any of these techniques to other methods that you may already use. Remember, if it works, it's right!

Pattern Making and Marking

Symmetrical and Mirror Image Designs

Before making your templates from either tag board or freezer paper, pattern direction needs to be addressed. Symmetrical designs are identical on either side of the center: If you placed a mirror down the exact center of the design lengthwise, the mirror would reflect the exact image on the other side. Or if placed in the center crosswise, the tops and bottoms would match. In appliqué patterns, you will often find that the design is symmetrical in its layout and all the shapes are the same, but certain pieces need to be reversed. This is true with pattern b that follows.

There are two identical leaves on either side of the stem, and the leaf template is the same for both leaves. However, when tracing onto the freezer paper, one leaf needs to be traced with the pattern or tag board template facing up, and the other needs to be traced in "reverse image." To do this, simply turn the pattern over and trace from the wrong side of the pattern, or turn the tag board template over and trace from the back side.

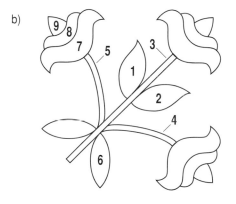

a)

Ohio Rose
a) Totally symmetrical

b)

Olde Tulip
b) Mirror image

You will need to get familiar with tracing reverse image or face up, as different uses of the freezer paper will affect the direction the design faces when completed.

Tracing

Patterns and templates for appliqué are the exact size of the finished piece, with no seam allowance added. When tracing your pattern for appliqué, you need to break apart the elements of the design. Do not trace the entire design as one unit and then try to cut it apart. It is difficult to keep perfect edges on both sides of a cut. Separate each unit of the design and draw it separately. *Do not add any seam allowances*.

a)

b)

Breaking apart the design, identifying by number

In using these techniques, the importance of accuracy and precision to the end product cannot be overemphasized. Trace your pattern pieces as carefully as you can. If tracing a line is difficult for you, make tag board templates to trace around. This reduces the amount of free-hand line tracing. Refer to page 83 for information on using a copy machine to print your lines for you.

Templates

Working With Freezer Paper

Freezer paper can be used in various ways to achieve the same end result.

Read through the methods presented here, and try each one before deciding which one will adapt to your particular project. Eventually you will use all the techniques, because they are adapted to specific problem areas in working with appliqué pieces.

Tag Board Templates

Make templates of the pattern pieces if multiples of each piece are needed. Tracing around a template is more accurate than tracing the pattern pieces individually several times. Identify each unit that makes up the design; you will need a template for each shape.

Trace shapes onto freezer paper

Trace each different pattern shape onto the paper side (the rough side) of the freezer paper. Do not add seam allowances at this time; trace only the shape that will be the finished appliqué. Do not cut the

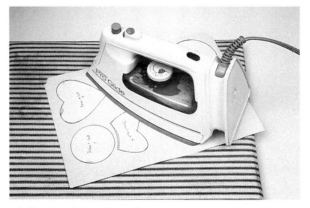

a) Press onto tag board

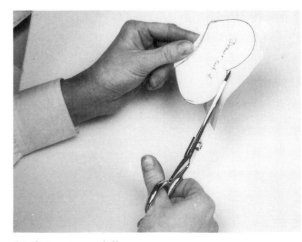

b) Cut out carefully

pattern out, but press the freezer paper onto a piece of tag board. Now cut the piece out on the line very carefully and accurately.

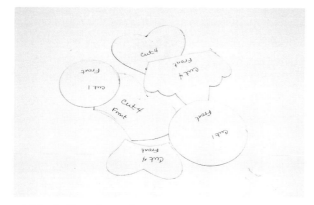

c) Mark "front" on pieces

Either mark "front" on the freezer paper as a reminder, or remember that this is the front side of the pattern. This is important, because some of the methods will have you working with a reverse image pattern, some will not, depending on which side of the freezer paper is exposed.

Freezer Paper Templates

If you do not have multiples to work with or you do not care to make permanent templates from tag board, you can simply trace each unit onto the freezer paper. You will need a separate freezer paper template for each unit in the design.

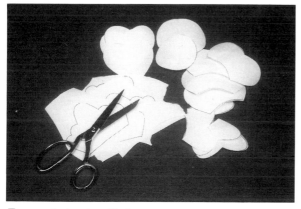

Freezer paper templates

Photocopy machines are a real timesaver in making patterns and templates. If you have one available to you, refer to Chapter Eleven for complete instructions.

Marking

Identify and mark the pattern for inside curves and inside points that will need to be clipped (see information on clipping below). Also do this for any seam allowances that act as extensions and will not be turned under, such as the ends of a stem or the inside curves of petals that a center sits on top of. These are extensions that are needed to rebuild the design. Mark the pattern with an "X" for each extension, and mark dash lines for each clipped area.

Pattern marked with "X" and clip lines

Grainlines

There are no particular grainline rules for placement of appliqué pieces, especially if the pieces are small and there will be quilting stitches on the surface of the appliqué. However, if the pieces are large or if no quilting will be on the surface, consider matching the grainline of the appliqué to the grainline of the background fabric. See the illustration below.

Grainlines to match background fabric

Grainline can also affect the ease of turning the edges over. You will find that bias is easier to turn under than are straight grain edges. For this reason it is helpful to place the pattern shapes with their longest part along the bias of the fabric.

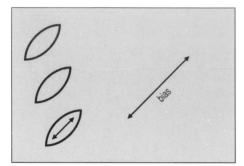

Bias and placement of edges

Handling Seam Allowances

Cutting

The seam allowance used in appliqué is ³⁄₁₆". This width gives the best results when turning the edges over. If your seam allowance is ¼" wide or wider, there is too much fabric to turn over, and the bulk turns into small pleats of fabric, creating points along the folded edge of the appliqué. Clipping of every edge is often necessary to let this extra bulk fit into the small space. If the seam allowance is less than ³⁄₁₆", or about ⅛", it is so small that handling will cause raveling, and laundering will fray the few threads left. A ³⁄₁₆" width is in between and seems to give a perfect edge without excess clipping or fraying. (Learning to eyeball this measurement will speed the cutting time considerably. View it as a fat eighth or a skinny quarter.)

Comparisons of ⅛", ³⁄₁₆", and ¼" seam allowances

Rough edges on the freezer paper templates or the tag board templates will produce appliqué shapes with the same rough edges. Cut exactly and use very sharp scissors for both paper and fabric. If you have difficulty with cutting, try keeping the scissors steady and move the fabric or paper through them. By turning the fabric or paper instead of the scissors, the blades keep constant tension and smoother cuts are developed.

Clipping

A basic guideline to prevent frayed edges is NEVER clip outside (convex) curves; only clip inside (concave) curves. If your seam allowances are too large, clipping is necessary, but too often the end result is pointed edges and frayed clips. The small seam allowance used here eliminates the need to clip outside curves. Inside curves, however, need to be clipped so that the fabric can expand to the larger area when turned under.

When clipping inside curves, clip the seam allowance only halfway to the freezer paper. Examine the grainline of the seam allowance, and try to make your clip on the bias grain of the seam allowance. This often results in a diagonal rather than a perpendicular clip. This also deters fraying.

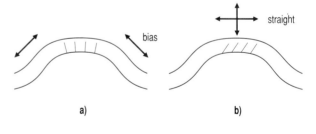

a) Clip on curved edge—straight cut
b) Clip on curved edge—diagonal cut

Inside points will also need to be clipped, as with hearts. One clip, straight down to within one thread of the paper, is all that is needed for inside points. *Do not overclip!*

Clip at inside point

Turning Smooth Edges

When rolling a ³⁄₁₆" seam allowance to the back side of an appliqué piece, care and a light touch are needed. Whether gluing or pressing the seam allowance into position, be careful to work with only small increments at a time, and treat the edge like pastry.

Beginning along a straight or slightly curved edge, gently roll the seam allowance over the freezer paper or tag board template edge, and pinch the glued edges together or press with the very tip of the iron. If gluing, use the very tip of your thumb and work only the very edge of the paper. Do not take large "bites" with your thumb, but instead, take tiny little pinches along the very edge of the paper. As you come to the curves, pinch and twist at the same time, again taking tiny bites with the tip of your thumb. (This will remind you of the pinch and twist motion used to make fluted pie crust.)

Gently roll seam allowance over paper edge

If pressing, try to finger-press the edges to form them before using the iron. Keep your fingers as close as you dare to the iron to control the edge. Take your time with this process.

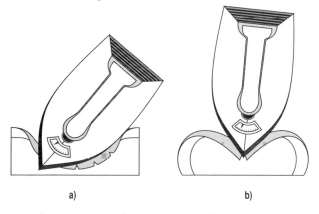

a) Iron edge pressing over seam allowance on curve
b) Iron edge pressing seam allowance at point

Perfect Points

When turning the edges over in preparation for stitching, points can be the most difficult area to handle. There are different ways of handling points, depending on the degree of the angle. Try different techniques on samples to master these tricky areas.

Method #1

Fold pointed end down onto the wrong side on the appliqué. If using freezer paper, be careful not to bend it over.

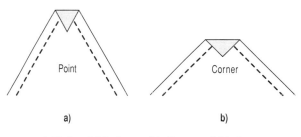

a) Point folded over b) Corner folded over

Press or glue the seam allowance over the point on the RIGHT-hand side of the piece.

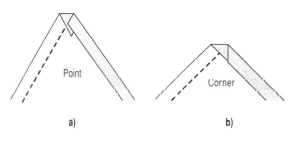

a) First edge folded over—point
b) First edge folded over—corner

Press seam allowance over the point on the LEFT-hand side of the piece.

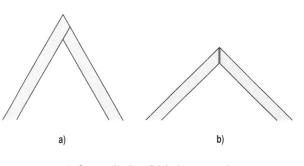

a) Second edge folded over point
b) Second edge folded over corner

Trim seam allowance as needed.

Method #2

Press or glue to the very end of the first side of the point or corner.

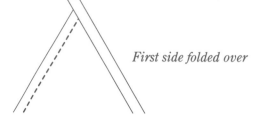

First side folded over

Press and glue the point over at a 45° angle, so that the point's seam allowance is over the left-side seam allowance. You might need to clip out some of the bulk of the point's seam allowance.

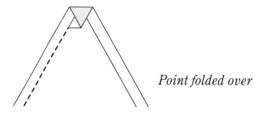

Point folded over

Press and glue the left seam allowance over. It is often helpful to use a pin or needle to fold the point over to keep it very pointed.

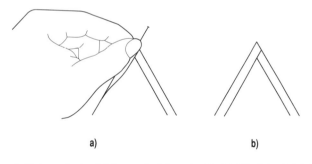

a)   b)

a) Using pin to fold over left-hand side b) Finished fold

TIP: *When working with small or slender shapes, it is helpful to trim the seam allowance to about 1/8" from paper's edge for ease in handling.*

Preparing Appliqué Pieces

Method #1—Glued Edges over Freezer Paper

This method uses a glue stick to secure the seam allowances. It gives a very secure edge for the presser foot to work with.

NOTE: *When using this method, the background fabric will need to be cut away within the stitched area for removal of the paper.*

1) For every unit needed for the design, make a tracing onto the rough side of the freezer paper. You need a freezer paper pattern for every piece of the design.

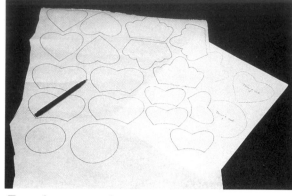

Traced pattern units

2) Cut out each pattern piece, being very careful that the cut edges are as smooth and even as possible.

Cut templates very carefully

3) Next, choose your fabrics. Refer to the information on grainlines before applying freezer paper to the fabric.

Space templates 1/2" apart

4) Place the fabric wrong-side-up on your iron-ing board.

TIP: *If your ironing board is heavily padded, you might find that a hard surface like a wood cutting board or piece of heavy cardboard allows the freezer paper to adhere more easily. Place the freezer paper templates plastic-side-down on the wrong side of the fabric. Leave ½" between each paper piece. Check grainline placement, if needed.*

5) Using a hot dry iron (cotton or linen setting), press the paper onto the fabric, being careful not to scorch the paper or the fabric. Scorching makes re-moval of the paper difficult, and it could damage your fabric. Be sure that the paper adheres firmly. If the pattern edges release, press firmly again.

Press templates to wrong side of fabric

6) With very sharp scissors, begin cutting around the shapes, adding ³⁄₁₆" seam allowance on all sides of the paper. Be careful not to let the seam allowance grow to ¼", because an extension this wide makes it difficult to turn the edge smoothly and evenly. A ³⁄₁₆" seam allowance eliminates the tucks and points on the edge as well as a lot of clipping that can later cause fraying of the appliqué edge.

Cut ³⁄₁₆" seam allowance on all sides

7) Before turning the edges under, look at the pattern pieces and identify what edges need to be clipped.

Clipping necessary areas

8) Using a fresh fabric-basting glue stick, apply a coating of glue to the seam allowance. Also apply glue the width of the seam allowance to the freezer paper. Following the guidelines in the instructions above, carefully roll the edges over to the paper side, using tiny pinch and twist motions with the tip of your thumb and forefinger.

a) Apply glue to seam allowance

b) Pinch seam allowances over edge

9) Turn the piece over and examine the edges. They should be smooth and perfect. Any unevenness or waviness along the edges is the result of poor paper cutting or rough handling of the paper edges when gluing and bending the paper over with the seam allowance. A lighter touch will prevent this. (You will improve with practice.) Now the pieces are ready for placement.

Smooth edge after turning

10) Once the stitching is done, the paper is removed. Cut the background fabric ¼" from the stitching around all the stitched pieces, dampen with water, and carefully remove the freezer paper.

a) Trim background fabric

b) Dampen paper

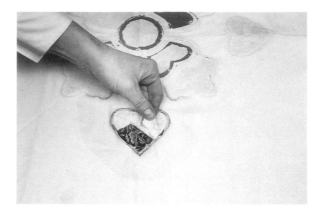

c) Pull paper out

d) Finished block

If using the Quilter's GluTube, follow instructions on the tube carefully. No water is needed to remove the paper with this product. Cut the background fabric away and gently pull it out. The glue will release when pulled.

Method #2—
Ironed Edges over Freezer Paper

This method eliminates the need for the glue stick. You press the edges over the paper edge and secure them by ironing them to the plastic side of the freezer paper. This method also eliminates the need to cut out the backing because the paper is removed before the design is completely sewn around.

1) Begin by reviewing the information on symmetrical designs and reverse image tracing. Make sure you understand how the position of the freezer paper on the fabric affects the final product. Because the plastic side of the paper faces you (not down), you will need to adjust your pattern directions. Prepare and trace the needed shapes onto freezer paper, one piece for each unit in the design.

2) Place the freezer paper onto the wrong side of the fabric, plastic side facing you. Pin securely in place, leaving ½" between each pattern piece.

Pin template—glossy side up—to fabric

3) Cut around each pattern, leaving a ³⁄₁₆" seam allowance.

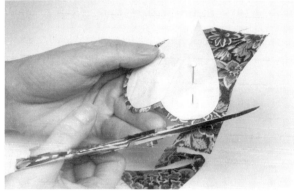

Cut seam allowance

4) Using the guidelines above, clip the necessary curves and points.

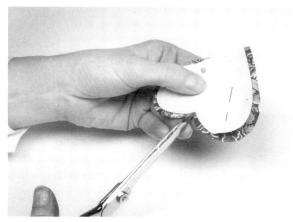

Clip points and curves

5) Using a hot dry iron, carefully ease the seam allowance over the edge of the freezer paper and press onto the plastic coating with the tip of the iron. This is where a small-pointed travel iron is very helpful.

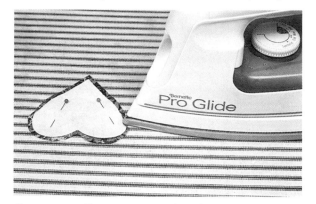

Ease seam allowance over edge of paper with iron

6) Remove the paper by pulling it out of an opening left during stitching. Because glue hasn't been used, the paper comes out easily. After the paper is removed, stitch closed the remaining opening.

Pull paper out from opening

Method #3—
Freezer Paper on Top of Fabric

A third choice with freezer paper is to apply it to the right side of the fabric, which makes paper removal the easiest. However, it is trickier to get smooth, even edges this way. Elly Sienkiewicz developed this technique for Baltimore style appliqué.

1) Iron freezer paper pieces onto the RIGHT side of the fabric, leaving ½" space between each pattern piece.

2) Cut out each piece, leaving ³⁄₁₆" seam allowance around all edges of the paper. Clip where necessary.

Template pressed onto right side of fabric

Cut seam allowances

3) Using a fresh glue stick, apply a film of glue on the wrong side of the seam allowance. Carefully roll the seam allowance over to the wrong side of the fabric. There will not be a paper edge to roll over this time. The paper is used as a guide line only. Take your time, and work with very small bits of fabric at a time. This edge is harder to achieve without the paper inside.

a) Apply glue to seam allowance

b) Turn edges over to wrong side

4) Leave the paper on until the piece is stitched in place. Then, the paper is easily removed from the top side.

a) Stitch over paper

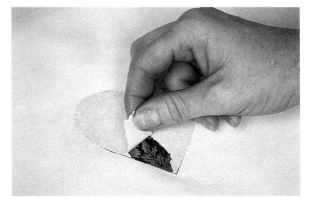

b) Pull paper off from top

Method #4—Tag Board Templates

Templates eliminate tracing individual pattern pieces onto freezer paper. Also, you end up with an appliqué piece that has no paper in it.

1) Trace the shape of each template onto the wrong side of your chosen fabric. (Several layers of fabric can be cut at one time when multiples are needed. Trace shape onto top layer only.)

Trace around tag board template

2) Cut ³⁄₁₆" to ¼" beyond the drawn line for seam allowances. (Because you will be working with an iron instead of your fingers and glue, the seam allowance may need to be wider than ³⁄₁₆" for ease in manipulation.)

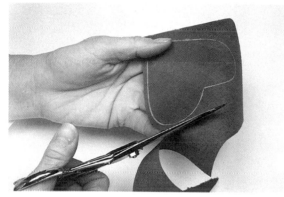

Cut seam allowance beyond line

3) Clip any necessary curves and identify the edges that will not be pressed over.

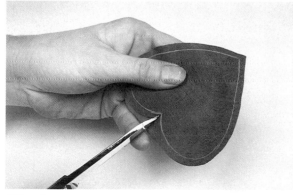

Clip where necessary

4) Spray a little spray starch into a small dish or the cap of the can. Place the appliqué piece wrong-side-up on the ironing board. Using your fingertip or a

small paintbrush, dampen the appliqué shape with starch along the seam allowance area.

Paint starch onto seam allowance

5) Lay the template on the fabric, aligning the drawn line with the cut edge of the template.

Reposition template

6) Using the side at the tip of a hot dry iron, ease the seam allowance over the template edge and press. Hold the iron on the seam allowance until the starch dries. The starch helps the edge become crisp and stay in place. Roll all edges over and press securely in the same manner.

Iron seam allowance over edge

7) Carefully remove the template and press again from the right side of the appliqué. The spray starch helps stiffen the edge so that the paper is not missed as a stabilizer when stitching.

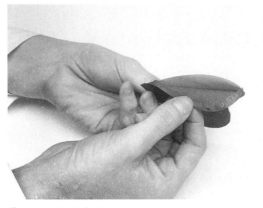

Remove template

Method #5—Stay Stitching

This is the original method that I taught years ago, and I still find that it is easy and appropriate in some cases.

1) Make a tag board template for each piece needed. Trace around the shape on the wrong side of the fabric. Do not cut the piece out yet.

Trace around template

2) With very small stitches, stay stitch on the traced line, going around the piece twice. This will give you a stiff seam to work with.

3) Cut ³⁄₁₆" to ¼" seam allowances beyond the stitching, around all sides of each piece (¼" may be easier to work with for this method).

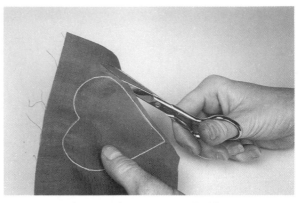

Cut seam allowance beyond stay stitching

4) Clip where needed, then roll and finger press or glue the seam allowances to the wrong side, using the stitched line as an edge. The stitching will be just inside the edge, on the wrong side. It should not show.

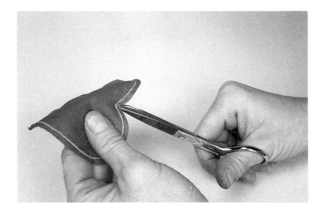

a) Clip where necessary

b) Finger press

Method #6—Aqua-Solv as a lining

Aqua-Solv is an excellent product for this method because it eliminates the bulk of another piece of fabric, and it disappears when it gets wet. This technique is easiest when used with larger, simple shapes.

1) Trace the desired designs onto Aqua-Solv. Do not add extension or seam allowances. (The water-erasable marking pen is good for this.)

Trace design onto Aqua-Solv

2) Place the Aqua-Solv on the right side of the appliqué fabric. With tiny stitches, machine straight stitch on the drawn line, leaving an opening large enough to turn the piece right-side-out.

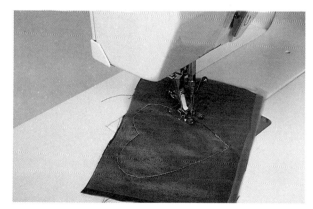

Stitch on line

3) Cut a ³/₁₆" seam allowance beyond the stitched line. Clip where needed.

TIP: I have found that cutting the seam allowance with pinking shears helps in obtaining a smooth edge when turning inside-out.

Cut seam allowance with pinking shears

4) Carefully turn the piece right-side-out, and finger-press the seam to smooth it and make it lie flat. If pressing is necessary, use only a dry iron on the fabric side.

5) Apply to background fabric and stitch in place. Remove Aqua-Solv by submerging in cold water.

Turn right side out

Bias Strips For Stems

Many appliqué patterns call for tiny stems. These can be difficult to do, using the above techniques. Bias methods of making stems of any size are given here. Choose the one that works best for you.

Find the true bias of the fabric by folding the corner over so that the crosswise grain lines up with the lengthwise grain (selvage). This will be true bias.

You generally do not use a width wider than ½". For ½" bias, cut bias strips 1¼" wide. For ¼" and narrower bias, cut strips ¾" wide. Anything narrower than a ¾" cut is very difficult to handle.

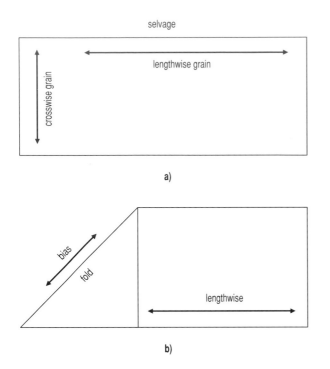

a)

b)

a) Grainline drawing b) Bias drawing

A very simple way to cut straight strips is to use a straight-edge ruler and a rotary cutter. If you find that the fabric moves too much, you can also use different widths of masking tape. Press the tape onto the bias of the fabric. Cut the strip along the edge of the masking tape. Carefully remove the tape after cutting. (Drafting tape is the easiest to remove.)

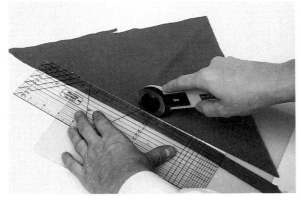

a) Ruler and rotary cutter

b) Masking tape

Method #1

1) After cutting the bias strip the desired width, fold the strip of bias in half lengthwise, wrong sides together.

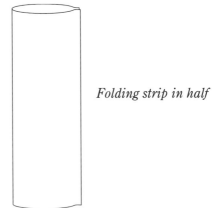

Folding strip in half

2) Stitch the folded strip down its length along the raw edge. The raw edge is on your right, the fold on the left.

NOTE: *The finished width of the stem is equal to the distance between this stitching and the folded edge.*

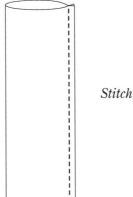

Stitch edge

3) Press, keeping the seam allowance in the center of the strip. Trim the raw edge, if necessary.

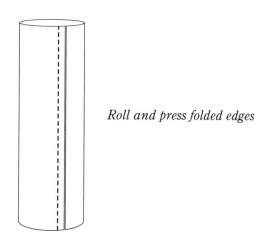

Roll and press folded edges

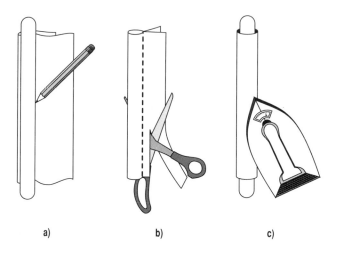

a) Bias bar—draw stitching line
b) Stitch and trim
c) Press with bar inserted

4) Stitch the folded edge down to the background fabric.

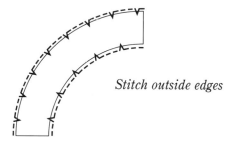

Stitch outside edges

Method #2—Bias Bars

Philomena Wiechek developed this method for her Celtic appliqué, and it is very successful.

1) Cut bias strip larger than the desired finished width, and fold it in half lengthwise, wrong sides together.

2) Lay the bias bar on top of the folded strip, one edge against the fold. Draw a line along the opposite edge for the seamline.

3) Stitch along the seamline. Trim excess seam allowance.

4) Slip the bias bar into the tube after stitching. Turn the tube so that the seam is centered down the length of the tube. Press the seam one direction. Trim seam allowance, if needed.

Method #3

This method was shared with me by Nina Stalschmidt and Ang Whittaker of Canada. It works well for both bias and straight grain strips and almost any size you need.

1) Cut strips slightly narrower than three times the finished width. Example: a ⅞" strip for a ⅜" finished stem.

2) Take a stitch with a pin into your ironing board cover. The size of the stitch is the desired finished size of the stem. Repeat with another pin, 3"–4" lower. (Do not use pins with a glass or plastic ball on the end.)

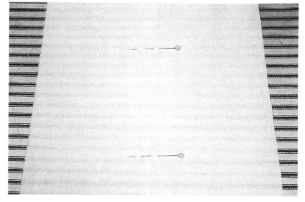

Pin placement on ironing board

3) Fold the end of the strip into thirds, one edge over the other. Thread under pins.

Fold and thread fabric strip under pin

4) As you pull the strip through the pins, the strip will automatically fold. Hold the strip on both ends as you draw it through the pins. Place the tip of your iron between the pins, and press as you pull the strip through. The point of the iron will just sit on the strip; you do not need to hold it.

Iron placed between pins, pull through

Method #4

This method allows you to make stems as small as ⅛". You will still need to work with ¾" wide bias and trim the excess away, once stitched in place.

1) Fold bias strip in half, lengthwise. Baste a line that is the needed finished width from fold to stitching.

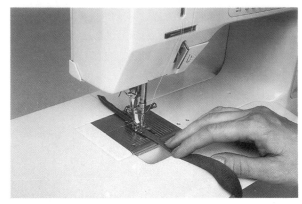

Fold strip and baste

2) Position and pin the basted strip onto the background. Lay the basted line along the outside curve if there is one, raw edges to the inside of the curve.

Position on background

3) Stitch just to the side of the basting, through the background fabric.

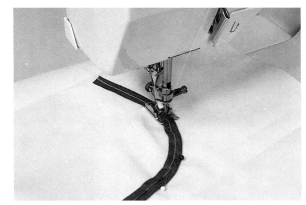

Stitch to background

4) Trim any excess seam allowance.

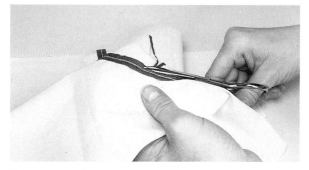

Trim seam allowance

5) Roll the bias over the seam allowance and appliqué the fold down.

Roll over and stitch edge

TIP: *When sewing your strips or stems onto the background, it is often easier to stitch the inner curve first. The bias will stretch along the outer curve when stitching down. This is less difficult than easing in the fullness of the inner curve after stretching the outer curve first.*

Building the Design

Once all the appliqué pieces are prepared, you are ready to build the design onto the background fabric. A lightbox is helpful for this process. I do not recommend drawing the placement lines onto the background fabric. Through the cutting and preparation stages, the pattern pieces are apt to change shape slightly and probably won't match the drawn lines exactly. The lightbox allows you to place the fabric on top of the pattern and see through the fabric for placement.

Prepare the background fabric by folding it into fourths, or any number of divisions needed, and press LIGHTLY with an iron. It is often helpful to also press in the diagonal centers. These lines are known as registration lines.

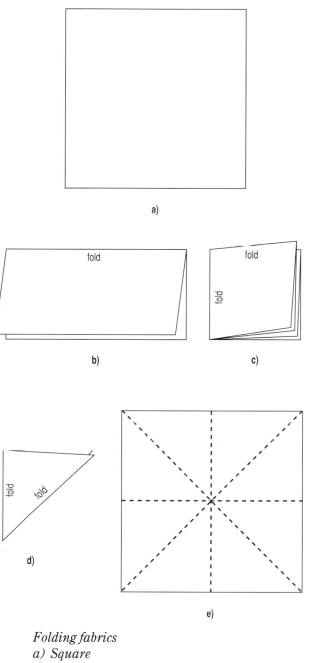

Folding fabrics
a) Square
b) Folded in half
c) Folded into fourths
d) Fourths folded diagonally
e) Unfolded square showing crease lines

If your pattern is in sections, you might want to prepare a full-scale layout of the finished design to use for placement. Mark the centering registration lines on the pattern to be used to line up with the background fabric.

Pattern with registration lines drawn in

Position the background fabric over the layout pattern, matching the registration lines, and tape or pin in place.

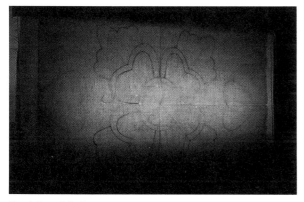
Position fabric on pattern

Beginning with the units that are in the most distant position—farthest away—begin placing and pinning each pattern piece to the background fabric. Using very thin pins like the Iris silk pins, pin along the edges. Place the pins perpendicular to the edge to

make them easy to remove while stitching. Use enough pins on each piece to prevent it from slipping or pivoting while stitching. A glue stick can be used, if you prefer.

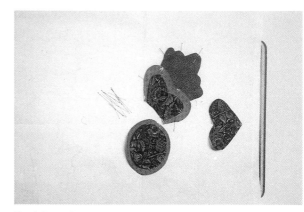
Position pieces on background and pin

Once the design is placed and secured, you can begin stitching. With machine work, the technique of placing one piece at a time and stitching it down before placing another is not advisable. If anything would slip from the pressure of the presser foot, it would not be known until another piece is ready to be positioned. The stitch techniques we are using are very difficult (if not impossible) to remove, making this risky.

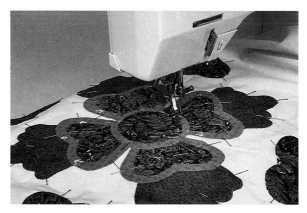
Stitch pieces in place

CHAPTER ELEVEN

The Magic of Photocopy Machines

I have saved hundreds of hours in preparation time by experimenting with copy machines. These wonderful tools can be a quilter's best friend, next to the sewing machine and the computer!

Find a machine that you can play with. We will be doing some unorthodox things with it, so it is best to have your own or use a friend's. Perhaps you know someone who has one in an office you can have access to. Don't be totally put off by purchasing one. The size you need is the desktop size, not a large, high-speed copier. You can now buy one at wholesale price clubs, used office supply businesses, etc. Check around, for I'm sure you'll see their value as you read on.

The copier needs to have a manual feed system. This is generally on the side opposite the paper tray. We will not be able to use the paper tray feed system for these techniques. Reduction and enlargement features are extremely valuable to a quilter. How many times have you needed a pattern or quilting design just slightly larger or smaller?

The following ideas are just a start. Experiment, and devise shortcuts the copier can do for you. So far, I have never jammed or harmed the machine with the ideas presented here. Just go slowly at first, and don't force the copier to do anything it doesn't accept readily.

Pattern-Making Tips Using the Photocopier

The most important use of the copier is reproductions. How many hours have you spent sitting and tracing the same design element over and over? And how accurate are you able to keep the pattern after tracing it that many times? Consider letting the copier do the reproductions for you, accurately and fast. If you are working with paper patterns to be used as basting templates, you can make copies normally. However, if you are hooked on freezer paper, the copier will print onto it, too! Here's how:

1) Cut the freezer paper to be the exact size of a sheet of copier paper.

2) Place the master pattern on the top of the machine. Place the freezer paper, plastic-coated-side-down, on top of a sheet of copier paper.

NOTE: If you run freezer paper through the machine by itself, the heat of the machine will alter the adhesion properties of the plastic.

3) Using the manual feed slot, slowly insert the two papers. The feeding rollers will pick up both and feed them through evenly. The master pattern will be printed onto the freezer paper.

4) Gently pull the two papers apart. (They will stick together slightly, but this does not affect the freezer paper's ability to stick to the fabric.)

Think of the timesaver this is when tracing hundreds of pie-shaped pieces for Drunkard's Path or Clamshells, or when making the same appliqué block 25 times for a full-size quilt.

Photocopying Directly Onto Fabric

Believe it or not, you can run fabric through the copier and achieve a screen-printed effect with the toner. First, the size of the project is limited to one thickness of fabric, at least one inch smaller on all sides than a sheet of copier paper. Secure the fabric to the paper with Scotch® Magic™ Tape. Use only this brand of tape because cellophane tapes melt in the machine. Tape around the edges of the fabric.

Tape fabric onto paper

Place the master you wish to copy on the top of the machine. Slowly insert the fabric/paper sheet into the manual feed slot.

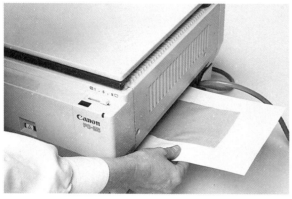

Feed paper into manual slot

When it appears on the other side, the master design is transferred onto the fabric, an exact duplicate. Heat-set the toner into the fabric with a press cloth and hot iron.

Think of the possibilities you have now! Consider making:

- Labels for the backs of your quilts—possibly from a business card or an original design you want to use.
- Care labels for products you make.
- Using Susan McKelvey's book, *Scrolls and Banners to Trace*, you can reproduce her antique designs directly onto muslin instead of tracing them.

TIP: If your copy machine has colored toner cartridges available, use the brown one for this technique to get an aged look.

To take this further, consider the copy machine in place of a hot iron transfer pencil. Instead of tracing the design over and over, run the fabrics through the copier and have the design line printed directly onto the fabric. You can do several of the same fabric at a time or several different units of the same block as with the Ohio Rose:

Hearts printed onto fabric

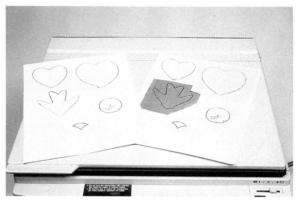

Several pieces of fabric copied at once

To do this, position the pattern pieces on the master paper. Lay another sheet of copier paper on top of the master, and position the appropriate fabrics directly on top of the pattern outline. Tape securely in place. As the fabric feeds into the machine, the lines will be printed directly on top of their corresponding fabrics.

Copy Machines and Wonder-Under

Because Wonder-Under is paper-backed, it can also be used with the copier. This is efficient when multiples of a design are needed. Simply fuse the Wonder-Under onto the wrong side of the fabric. Secure the fused fabric to a sheet of paper with Scotch Magic Tape. *Do not remove the paper backing of the Wonder-Under.* Insert into the manual feed slot of the copier. Cut out the design, then remove the web's paper backing.

Photocopying Fabric for Designing

I was first introduced to this idea by Jinny Beyer in a color class she was teaching. She passed out stacks of "paper fabric" that had been made by photocopying her designer fabrics. As we worked with the papers, the importance of value to a quilt became apparent.

Fabric can be placed directly onto the top of a copy machine and "photographed." The result is a gray reproduction of the print. The value is picked up through the gray and is comparable to working with a gray scale. This is often useful in planning scrap quilts, where the value of the fabric is as important, if not more so, than the actual color. Each fabric will photocopy differently, based on its value.

By copying many different fabrics of various print scales, pattern repeats, values, etc., you can design quilts without regard to color.

Photocopied fabric

CHAPTER TWELVE

Machine Preparation and Stitching

Mock Hand appliqué is an instant gratification experience. The preparation is the most time-consuming part of the process. Once your pieces are ready to stitch, the hard work is finished. You will be amazed at how fast you can stitch your appliqués, and how much your machine stitching will resemble the finest of hand work.

Machine Set-Up

Start by threading the machine. The bobbin must be wound with 60 weight/2-ply or 80 weight/2-ply fine machine embroidery thread. Make sure that the thread winds tightly and evenly onto the bobbin. Thread the invisible nylon on the top of the machine. Refer to page 11 for threading guidance. Use a size 60/8 or 65/9 needle. The smaller the needle, the more control of the tension you have.

Mock Hand appliqué utilizes the sewing machine's ability to do blind stitching for hems. With some minor adjustments, this stitch can be used to duplicate the look of hand blind stitching. Begin by locating the blind stitch on your stitch selector dial or panel: it does 4–7 straight stitches on the right, then zigzags to the left. Any other stitch will not have the same invisible appearance. Program the machine to blind stitch.

Blind stitch

If your machine does not have a blind stitch, or the width of the stitch is not adjustable, you might want to experiment with a tip passed on by Barbara Eikmeier. She uses the darning foot and works free motion. The machine is set for straight stitching instead of a blind stitch. She manually creates the stitch needed by taking two stitches forward, beside the folded edge, then moves the fabric sideways for the tiny zigzag needed to secure the appliqué. Once the zigzag is made, another two stitches are made forward, then one sideways. This eliminates the need to pivot and turn the fabric, making complicated pieces or large bulky quilt tops much more manageable. However, you will need to practice quite a bit to obtain the control to achieve accurate stitching.

Many machines automatically put the needle in the right-hand position. If this is the case, leave it there. The machine will make a nicer stitch in this position.

Now, fine-tune the machine so that this stitch becomes an appliqué stitch instead of a hemming stitch. Begin by sewing a line of these stitches on a scrap of fabric. Notice how far apart they are and how wide the zigzag bite is. Reduce the stitch width to a little narrower than "1". The stitch width should be just wide enough to barely catch 2 to 3 threads of the appliqué fabric. A stitch that is too wide will show and spoil the effect, and one too narrow will not hold the appliqué in place.

Next, adjust the stitch length. It will be a bit shorter than "1" on most machines, or approximately 25 to 30 stitches to the inch. The distance between the stitches needs to be ⅛" or slightly shorter. If too much space is left between the stitches, there will be gaps along the edge of the appliqué.

The tension will need to be adjusted because of the extremely short stitch length being used. Start by reducing the top tension slightly. If further adjustments need to be made, refer to page 30, Chapter Four in the Satin Stitch unit for detailed information on tension adjustments.

TIP: *If you are using a Bernina, be sure to thread the bobbin thread through the hole in the finger of the bobbin case. This will automatically tighten your bobbin tension.*

It is not unusual to need to tighten the bobbin tension. You may also have to loosen the top slightly to keep the bobbin thread from showing on the top. If you plan to do a lot of this type of sewing, consider purchasing another bobbin case and keeping it tight, using the other case for normal sewing. Test the stitches again, and make sure that NO bobbin thread is showing on the top of the piece.

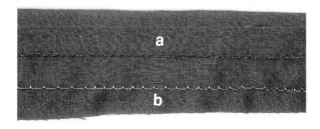

a) Proper tension b) Poor tension

If there is nothing you can do to prevent the bobbin thread from showing, matching the bobbin thread in size 60 weight/2-ply to the background fabric will help alleviate the problem.

Put the open-toe appliqué foot on the machine. This foot allows you to see the stitches clearly as they are being made. If the needle is in the right needle position, you will be able to guide off the inside edge of the right toe of the presser foot.

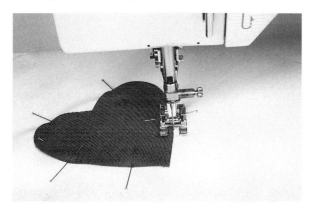

Center needle position

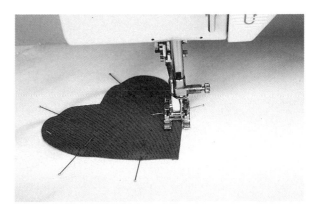

Right needle position

Practice using this tiny stitch on samples before attempting to stitch your project. You need to train your eyes to do the close work of keeping the needle exactly off the edge of the appliqué, making sure that the zigzag catches the appliqué with every bite.

Fold a piece of fabric and place this fold on another piece of fabric, simulating an appliqué on a background square. Align the needle in its right-hand position so that it virtually rubs the fold while stitching. *Do not let the straight part of the stitch catch any part of the appliqué.*

Needle in straight mode beside edge

When the needle swings to the left, the appliqué will be caught. Keep your eye on the needle at all times

Needle in left swing on edge

as it stitches straight. Go slowly so that you have control.

Practice corners and points to learn to make sure stitches secure the points and corners on both sides and on the actual point.

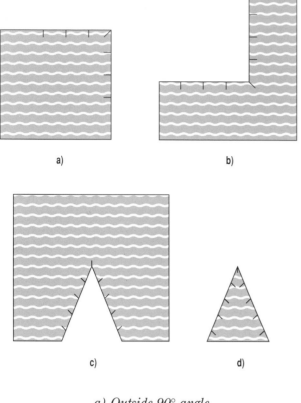

a) b)

c) d)

a) Outside 90° angle
b) Inside 90° angle
c) Outside 45° angle
d) Inside 45° angle

To lock off the stitches, come back around to the beginning and stitch over the beginning stitches for ¼". These stitches are so tight and small that they are very unlikely to pull out. In fact, you will not want to have to take any of them out if you make a mistake. Sometimes it is easier to start over!

When working on multiple layers of the design, stitch the layers together before placing the pieces on the background fabric. An example of this is one heart on top of another: Stitch the small heart onto the larger heart first, then apply to the background fabric. This makes the job of removing the freezer paper much easier. If all the layers are sewn on top of each other through to the base fabric, you will later have to dig paper out of the very small channels, which is tedious and sometimes unsuccessful. Also, the appliqué will have a flat, stiff look.

Stitch layers together first

Once you have your machine set to produce exactly the stitch you want, make note of the machine settings in your manual or notebook. Also make note of the top and bottom tension settings. Now you have no excuses not to produce all those wonderful appliqué projects you just know you would never get done by hand!

CHAPTER THIRTEEN

Putting Theory Into Practice

Now that you have read through pages and pages of instruction, put it to use by practicing with the following Love Tulip pattern. Follow the directions step by step and you will end up with a lovely 12" appliqué square. You will use the freezer paper template method which involves gluing the edges to the back side.

Begin by identifying the units of the pattern on page 93: There are two different hearts, two leaves, a stem, two different petals, and a bud. You will need a freezer paper pattern for every piece, i.e.: 1 small heart, 1 large heart, 1 stem, 2 leaves, 1 large petal, 1 small petal, and 1 bud. Trace the units individually from the pattern onto freezer paper.

Press freezer paper onto fabrics

Cut out the fabric, leaving a 3/16" seam allowance around all the edges.

Trace units onto freezer paper

For a further shortcut, refer back to page 83, Chapter Eleven for information on using a photocopy machine to produce freezer paper patterns.

Once the tracing is finished, cut out the freezer paper patterns as carefully as you can. On the wrong side of the fabrics, iron the freezer paper down securely. Leave ½" between all the pattern pieces.

Cut seam allowances

Next, examine the shapes to see where you will need to clip:

1) At the cleavage of the hearts, make one clip straight down to the paper.

2) The deep inside curve of the leaves and petals will need to be clipped with tiny clips that go halfway to the paper.

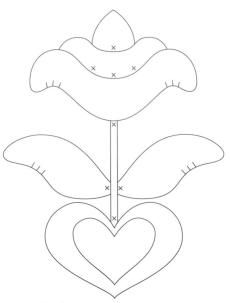

Marks for each pattern piece

Identify the edges that will not get turned under. In this pattern, there are six of these edges. They are:
1) the ends of the 2 leaves
2) the bottom edge of the bud
3) the bottom edge of the small petal
4) the 2 ends of the stem

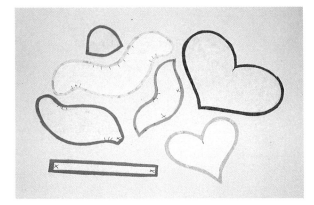

Edges not to be turned marked with "X"

Turn all the remaining edges under, using the techniques discussed on page 70. Be very careful to keep the edges as smooth as possible, free of points and pleats.

TIP: *When turning the edge over the tips of the leaves and large petal, trim the seam allowance to ⅛" if necessary. This gives you less bulk to try to fit into a small space. Using very tiny pinches with the very tips of your fingers, twist slightly as you turn the seam allowance over and pinch. This will ease the fullness in. On curves like this, it is often helpful to start in the center and work out each direction to ease in fullness. By the time you have done all eight of these*

elements, you will feel more comfortable with them.

Before placing the pattern pieces on the base fabric, align the small heart on top of the large heart and appliqué in place.

Stitch small heart onto large heart

TIP: *When stitching into the inside points as at the top of the heart, manually control the machine feed so that you can make sure that there are adequate bites of the zigzag stitch to hold down the point, as shown above. This can also be achieved by shortening the stitch length. Once out of this area, return to the longer stitch length.*

Background on light box—crease positioned on line

Position all pieces and pin

Now, pin the pattern pieces in place onto a 12 ½" square of base fabric. It can be positioned either diagonally or straight. Simply lay the base fabric on top of the pattern, aligning the crease lines with the pattern for centering, and position the pieces. Use very fine pins and pin securely to the base fabric.

I would suggest stitching around the leaves first. When stitching, take your time and concentrate on the needle being as close to the edge of the appliqué as possible without stitching on top of the edge. This way, the stitching will be invisible and the swing stitch will just barely show. Pivot as necessary to control the curve. To pivot, stop with the needle in the fabric when in the right position, and move the fabric slightly to realign the edge with the needle. Do this as many times as necessary to keep the needle in proper alignment. Refer to page 41, Satin Stitch Unit, Chapter Five for more information on pivoting around curves.

Next, stitch the stem, the bud, then around the petals. As you come to the tips of the large petal, slow down and carefully pivot around the curve. Make sure that several swing stitches are catching the appliqué so that the tiny seam allowance won't have a chance of fraying out. These are fragile areas and usually the first to fray, so pay special attention to them.

Once you have finished the flower, stitch the large heart, making sure that you anchor the inside point at the top of the heart. When all the stitching is completed, turn the block over and carefully cut the base fabric away, cutting inside the stitching lines ¼". When you have removed the base fabric of the large heart, gently tear the freezer paper from inside the stitching of the small heart. Now cut ¼" inside this stitching line (you will be cutting the large heart fabric this time). This exposes the paper inside the smaller heart.

All backs removed

After cutting the backing, either submerge the whole block in warm water, or use a spray bottle and wet the seam allowance areas—anywhere the glue stick was used. Water will dissolve the glue. Gently peel the paper out of the appliqué pieces. The freezer paper should roll out easily if it is wet enough.

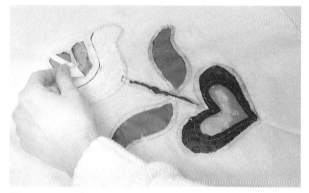

Dampen and remove paper

NOTE: If you have chosen to use the GluTube, no water is necessary to remove the paper.

Blot the block dry, and press from the back side of the block. Use a permanent press setting on your iron.

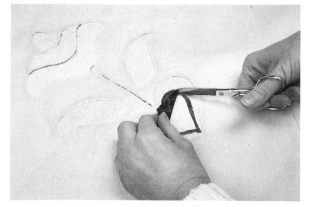

Removing layers of fabric and paper

Finished block, back and front side

Congratulations! When you turn the block over, you will be delighted at how beautiful the stitching is—just like, and sometimes better than hand stitching. You will also be pleased with the durability of this technique. Now appliqué quilts are as easy as strip piecing! Try Hawaiian Quilting with this method; the results are beautiful.

If this technique has inspired you about the possibilities, read on. It gets better!

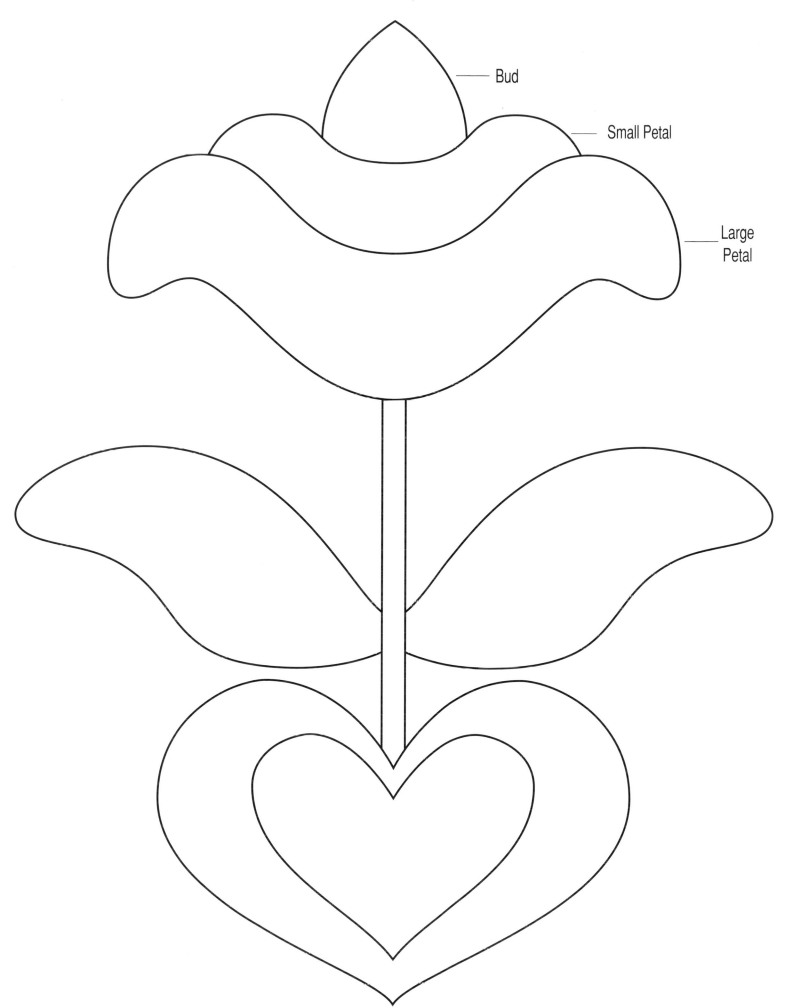

Bud

Small Petal

Large
Petal

Once Were What Vices are Now Habits by Gail Garber. This was an invitational challenge quilt made for the Silver Dollar City National Quilt Festival. Gail selected the name because when she first learned this technique in 1983, all the stitching was done by hand. In this quilt every stitch, including the quilting, was done on her machine—in record time.

Broderie Perse by Phyllis Freerksen. Fabric cutouts were applied to the background fabric using blanket stitching.

PART THREE

More Hand Reproduction Techniques

CHAPTER FOURTEEN

Straight Stitch Appliqué

NOTE: *We use the same preparation methods for these techniques that we used for Mock Hand appliqué. Review Chapter Ten for instructions on preparing templates and pattern pieces.*

Straight stitch appliqué has been used on quilts to achieve beautiful, durable appliqué since the early 1860's. This method provides a very sturdy edge, with visible stitching, but it does not have the heavy, bulky feel of Satin Stitch appliqué. The technique involves folding the edge over, as with Mock Hand appliqué.

Some pattern adaptations are helpful in preparing the pieces for stitching. It will be easiest to prepare the edges if you slightly round any sharp inside corners and create gentle curves. See the illustration below.

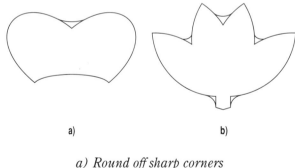

a)   b)

a) Round off sharp corners
b) Create gentle curves

You can use any of the techniques discussed in Chapter Ten to prepare the pattern pieces. Your choice will be determined by whether you want to cut the backs out, how detailed the pattern pieces are, etc. After experimenting with the various options, you will know which one suits the pattern you are working on.

The following brief instructions are for working with the template and spray starch method. The LoveTulip pattern given on page 93 or any pattern of your choice can be used to work through this technique.

Trace pattern pieces onto freezer paper. The line that is drawn and cut from the freezer paper will represent the finished edge of the appliqué itself, so accuracy is extremely important. Make note of the pieces that need to be cut in reverse if your pattern is not symmetrical. Iron the freezer paper onto tag board and cut on lines. (See Chapter Ten for further instructions).

Following the guidelines for grainline on page 67, place the templates on the wrong side of the fabric. Leave at least ½" between each piece of paper. Trace around each shape, repeating as often as needed for the design.

Carefully cut ³⁄₁₆" to ¼" seam allowances on all sides of the traced line. Clip points and inside curves, and identify edges that will be under another piece and not turned over.

NOTE: *The width you cut the seam allowance is determined by your ability to work with the point of the iron over a template edge. The narrower the seam allowance, the nicer the edge, but the more difficult it is to work with when using an iron. Experiment until you can get the edge you want.*

Lay the pieces on the ironing board wrong-side-up, and position the template within the traced lines. Using your fingertip or a paintbrush, apply spray starch to the seam allowances and press over the edge of the template. Press until dry.

TIP: *Press sharp points first, then concave (inside) areas, then straighter areas. Continue this until all seam allowances—except edges that are extensions—are pressed over. Carefully remove the templates and press again from the front side of the appliqué. The edges should be smooth and crisp.*

If you have trouble getting circles and near circular shapes smooth and even, try this: Using thread that matches your fabric, carefully sew (by machine or hand) a line of gathering stitches in the seam allowance. This will help distribute the extra fullness in the seam allowance when it is turned over. Place the template on the shape, and pull up the gathering thread. Evenly distribute the fullness and press. Carefully remove the template.

Gathering stitch in seam allowance

Gathering up around template

Prepare base fabric by folding in half lengthwise, crosswise, then diagonally, and pressing lightly to place registration lines. Center this block over the pattern and begin placing the pattern pieces where they belong. Pin securely, or use spots of glue stick to hold in place.

Prepare your sewing machine by threading the top and bobbin with matching thread. You can use regular 100% cotton mercerized sewing thread (50 weight/3-ply) or machine embroidery threads (30, 50, or 60 weight), depending on your personal preference. Invisible nylon can also be used if you like its appearance. Experiment. Use the needle size appropriate for the thread you choose. Refer to Chapter One, page

14, in the Satin Stitch unit for a helpful chart.

You have a choice of machine feet to work with for this method. You can either use the open-toe appliqué foot that we have been using up to now, or you can change to an edge stitching foot, if one is available for your machine. This foot resembles the blind stitch foot, but does not have the easement bar across the center. The guiding bar is kept next to the edge of the appliqué, and the needle position is adjusted to where you desire the stitch to be placed along the edge. (If your machine is a Bernina, this is foot #10.)

Edge stitch foot

The stitch is sewn from the folded edge of the appliqué piece, approximately 1/16". Adjust the needle position of the machine to the distance you prefer. Use your straight stitch throat plate instead of the normal zigzag plate. Your machine makes a nicer straight stitch and gives you accuracy in pivoting and easing. Set the stitch length for 12 stitches per inch, or between 2 and 2 1/2. Sew a sample to check tension settings and stitch length before stitching the appliqué.

Starting with the pieces farthest away from you, stitch along the edge of the appliqué. Go slowly around curves and points, keeping the stitch distance from the edge as exact and even as you can. Pivot when necessary. Change color of thread when fabric color changes. Lift the appliqué piece on top of the piece you are stitching, and begin the stitching at that piece's raw edge.

Lift edge of top piece

Continue around and end at its raw edge. Repeat this for each additional layer. When the next layer is stitched, it will catch and hold the thread tails of the lower piece. On the very top piece, either do a short backstitch, make several tiny short stitches, or take the threads to the back and secure by tying and adding a small drop of Fray Check®.

CHAPTER FIFTEEN

Blanket Stitch Appliqué

Blanket stitched or buttonhole stitched appliqué was very popular in the early 1900's, especially in the 1920's and 1930's. We have all seen Sun Bonnet Sue quilts appliquéd with black thread, the blanket stitch securing the raw edge to the base fabric.

Blanket stitched appliqués by machine use a raw edge, making preparation easier, but with the techniques presented here, you will not have to work with fusibles and interfacings as with satin stitch. This leaves the texture of the appliqué soft and puffy like hand work, not stiff and flat as with fusibles. You will find a multitude of places to use this technique.

With computerized sewing machines, almost any hand stitch can be reproduced by machine. The blanket stitch is no exception. It takes one stitch forward, then swings to the left, and back to the right, the needle hitting the same hole on both swings. Then one stitch forward again, and a repeat of the side swings.

Blanket stitch illustration

If you have this stitch on your machine, program it and start to play. Sew a few stitches as the machine

Various blanket stitch sizes

is programmed, then adjust the width and length of the stitch to suit your tastes. (The ability to infinitely adjust the width and length is ideal.) Some people like this edge finish to be bold and large; others prefer it to be delicate and small.

If you do not have a blanket stitch on your machine, use the blind hem stitch used for Mock Hand appliqué. To obtain the look of the blanket stitch, use two threads on the top of the machine, instead of only one. The two threads, which will actually be four after stitching over and back, will fill in the "V" part of the hem stitch, making it resemble the blanket stitch.

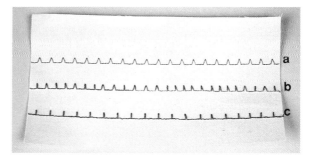

*a) Regular blind hem b) Blind hem with two threads
c) Results from manually retaining fabric*

If the "V" does not fill in sufficiently using two threads, manually hold the fabric from moving forward when the right swing of "V" is stitched. This will allow the needle to take the second needle swing in the same hole as the first, giving you a perfect blanket stitch. With practice this will be easy.

If you have the triple elastic stitch or point de Paris stitch on your machine, see if it is an acceptable substitute for a true blanket stitch. This stitch will appear heavier because it stitches straight forward, backward, forward, side, side.

The Blanket Stitch technique is a raw edge finish, so preparation is different than for the previous methods given. Because everyone tends to approach this technique differently, I've included three preparation methods. Try all of them, then decide which works best for you.

Method #1

I was first introduced to this method at the 1989 Vermont Quilt Festival when Jeanne Hutchinson of Northfield, Vermont, used it on the raffle quilt. She chose to work with an antique pattern called Oriental Poppy, dating back to 1871. The original quilt was found as a fragment in a hope chest and was reproduced by Rose Kretsinger in the early 1930's. This original reproduction can be seen in *The Romance of the Patchwork Quilt in America* by Carrie A. Hall and Rose G. Kretsinger. The pattern was later published in the April 1980 issue of *Quilters Newsletter Magazine*. Jeanne's quilt, named Festival Poppy Orientale, can be seen on the back cover of most 1990 issues of *Quilter's Newsletter Magazine*. It is a very close replication of the original.

When Jeanne first explained how she achieved the stitched effect, I couldn't wait to go home and try it. She used tiny strips of fusible hem tape laid over the cutting line which had been transferred onto the wrong side of the fabric. Once the tape is fused in place and the pattern pieces cut out, there is a tiny edge of fusible available to bond to the background fabric. This allows the edge to be stable and secure while stitching, but leaves the rest of the appliqué piece loose and soft as in hand appliqué. (See photos at right.)

Method #2

This process can be time-consuming, and I didn't get far with it. In October, 1989 while at Quilt Market, I discovered a new product called Thread Fuse®. I reconsidered the possibilities of making an Oriental Poppy quilt, and this is an alternative method of preparing appliqué pieces for Blanket Stitching.

1) Make hot iron transfer patterns of the pattern shapes (refer to Chapter Three, page 23 or trace from templates. This time we will be stamping the designs onto the right side of the fabric, so be aware of reverse image tracings if your pattern is not symmetrical. (Refer to page 65 for information).

TIP: The photocopy machine process on page 83 is faster and more accurate.

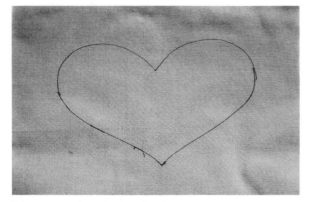

Lines transferred onto fabric

Placing fusible strips over line

Press in place

Cut on line

Mock Hand Appliqué & Other Techniques

11) Baltimore Beauty by Barbara Trumbo. Barbara used patterns from Elly Sienkiewicz's books, using freezer paper and Mock Hand appliqué techniques.

12) Detail of Various Techniques

14) *Johann Hieronymous Kapsburger—I'm Sorry I Missed your Concert* by Susanne Meyer Rasmussen. Decorated Christmas tree, hand and machine quilted, machine appliquéd. Sue was unable to figure out how to include a strand of lights in a quilt. While at a concert, she closed her eyes and designed the entire piece. At the intermission, she drew it on a piece of paper.

13) *Lone Star.* This Lone Star quilt was the 1991 raffle quilt for Konza Prairie Quilt Guild of Manhattan, Kansas. It was designed and constructed by Barb Eikmeier and Dorine Elsea. The Mock Hand appliqué was stitched by Barb, the piecework by Dorine. The quilt was hand quilted by members of the KPQG. The patriotic theme and yellow ribbon were incorporated into the design in support of the military who were serving in the Persian Gulf. Quilt owned by JoAnne Bair, Lincoln, Nebraska.

15) *Winter Girl* stitched by Kathy Perry. Kathy found Mock Hand appliqué so simple to master that after class she chose this Piecemakers pattern as her first project. Although stitched and quilted by machine, it looks hand done.

16) *Perennially Spring* by Linda Mann. This quilt is an original design using an adaptation of Nancy Pearson's Morning Glory appliqué. It was made for a quilt challenge requiring at least one 9-patch on the face of the quilt. A 9-patch was sewn into two of the leaves to meet this requirement.

17) Lancaster Rose Pillow. Made by Barbara Blum in her beginning appliqué class.

18) Magic Flower Vest by Mace McEligot. Blind stitch appliqué was used to apply the flowers, stems and leaves. The vest is quilted with twin needles and decorative stitch patterns.

19) Sforzinda by Susanne Meyer Rasmussen. Made for a quilt challenge. The fabrics were purchased sight unseen. Upon completion, the colors reminded Sue of the colors and designs of the Renaissance architecture in Florence, Italy. "Sforzinda" is a Renaissance term describing a complete architectural model of a city or palace.

Mock Hand Appliqué and Other Techniques

21) Attic Windows and Santas in the Forest
Designed and made by Donna Fite McConnell. The 2½″ mini log cabin blocks are enhanced with delicate blanket stitched miniature appliqués.

20) I Remember Santa Skating on Mistletoe Pond by Sandy Jones. Original pattern by Hickory Hollow. Mock Hand appliqué and machine quilting techniques were used.

*22) **Ohio Rose*** by Harriet Hargrave. Mock Hand appliqué techniques were used to reproduce the 1930's classic. Machine quilting and 100% cotton batting were used to finish the top.

Mock Hand Appliqué and Other Techniques

23) Tulips by the Path by the author. Made from a pattern from The Stitch Connection. Appliqué techniques, used to create the appliqué and curved pieces, made it possible to complete the top in seven hours.

24) Sunbonnet Sue. Sharon Binder used a Little Quilts pattern and 1930's reproduction fabric. Sharon blanket stitch appliquéd each Sue with black thread to keep with the 1930's feel.

25) Rose Garden by Patty Albin. Using a pattern from Curved Two Patch System, Patty used appliqué techniques to create the curves for each rose.

26) Eagles Over Colorado. Patty Albin used curved piecing à la appliqué to design and stitch this piece using Drunkard's Path blocks. Inspired by a quilt made by Mary Jo Dalrymple.

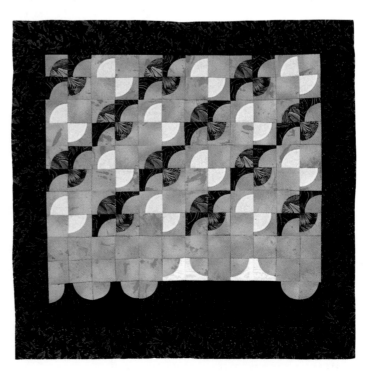

Mock Hand Appliqué and Other Techniques

29) *Catamaran* by Mace McEligot. An original design using her own hand-dyed and marbleized fabrics. Mace stitched the bias using the blanket stitch.

28) *The Rose* by Cathy Robiscoe. Cathy's method of reverse appliqué achieves a detailed leaded glass piece without using bias tape. Original design by Cathy.

27) *Untitled* by Gail Garber. Traditional Stained Glass design of unknown origin. Polished cottons and cotton solids used with bias tape method.

30) Zia by Gail Garber. This sunburst design was done as a color study. Gail used colors she was unaccustomed to working with. The print was added to bridge the gap from yellow to gold. A "Zia" is the New Mexico sun symbol.

31) Complex Floral Swag Border by Jeanna Kimball. Blanket stitched by the author. Taken from Jeanna's book, *Appliqué Borders, An Added Grace*. Blanket stitching makes small details easiest to achieve by machine.

32) Cathedral Window by Linda Eckblad. Machine stitching makes this fast and easy.

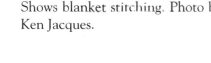

34) *Detail of Stars and Flowers.*
Shows blanket stitching. Photo by
Ken Jacques.

33) *Stars and Flowers* by Sharyn Craig. Appliqué
stitched using blanket stitch technique. Photo by
Ken Jacques.

35) *Windflower* by Sharyn Craig
and Arlene Stamper. A 1992
Visions raffle quilt—machine
pieced, machine appliquéd and
quilted. Photo by Ken Jacques.

36) *At Home* by Nancy Barrett. Taken from an original pen and ink drawing by an Oklahoma City artist, all the elements of the house and its setting were appliquéd using the blanket stitch. In some cases the shapes of the pieces required free motion technique. Occasionally Nancy used the wrong side of a fabric to create a particular effect; i.e., the darkest "shingle" fabric when turned over was perfect for shadows on other sections of the roof. When Nancy was finished with the appliqué, she then painted all the details with acrylics. The corners of the picture frame are appliquéd with a standard satin stitch. Photo by Randy Taylor.

37) *Details of At Home*
Photo by Randy Taylor.

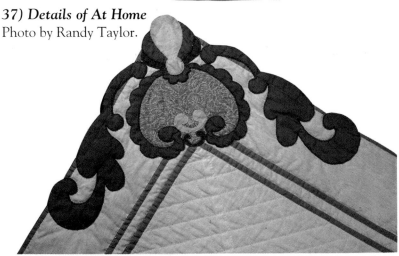

2) Fill a bobbin with Thread Fuse. This thread is used only in the bobbin, so you will be stitching from the right side of the fabric. This is why the design needs to be on the right side.

3) Thread the top of the machine with matching embroidery thread or invisible nylon.

4) Place a piece of paper under the appliqué fabric. This will be used as a stabilizer. Using your darning foot for difficult shapes or your open-toe foot for simple shapes, stitch slightly to the inside of the transfer line, through the paper.

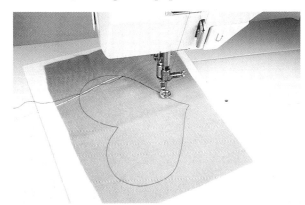

Stitching with darning foot

5) Once stitched, gently tear off the paper, and carefully cut right outside the stitching, from the wrong side. Handle these pieces gently, as they can fray easily at this stage.

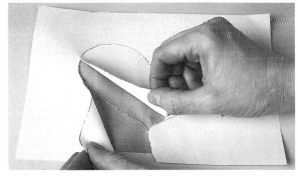

Remove paper carefully

Cut close to stitching

6) Using your pattern for layout placement, position the pattern and base fabric on the ironing board or any large ironing surface. Position the appliqué pieces and press with a hot iron. The Thread Fuse will bond to the base fabric, keeping the edges secure and the piece in place. Once all pieces are positioned and bonded, you are ready to stitch.

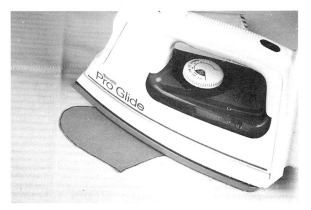

Press pieces onto background fabric

Method #3

Thread Fuse works well with print fabrics, but the straight stitching tends to show through the blanket stitching when using solids. The following technique was developed to alleviate this.

Using Wonder-Under or HeatnBond, trace the appliqué design onto the paper side of the fusible. Check whether you need to trace in reverse or not.

Trace designs onto paper side of fusible

Cut the fusible ⅛" to ³⁄₁₆" inside of the line you have drawn. You will be cutting the center of the appliqué design away. Do not cut on the line.

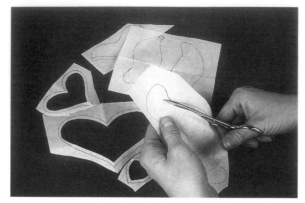

Cut ³⁄₁₆" inside drawn line

Fuse the tracing to the wrong side of the appliqué fabric.

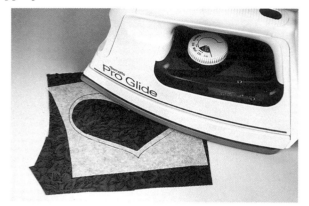

Fuse onto appliqué fabric

Carefully cut along the drawn line, keeping the edges smooth.

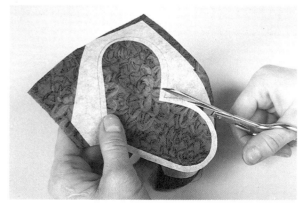

Cut carefully on drawn line

Gently and carefully tear paper off the fusible left along the edge.

Remove paper from edge

You now have a "bead" of fusible ⅛" to ³⁄₁₆" wide on the very edge of the appliqué. This will fuse the edges firmly but will leave the appliqué soft and free, ready to stitch. I found this to be an efficient technique that also prevented frayed edges from too much handling.

Again, try all three methods and pick your favorite.

Threads

Experiment with threads to find the ones that give your edge the look you desire. I found that the fine machine embroidery threads such as Mettler 60/2 and DMC 50/2 were too fine and tightly twisted to cover the raw edge sufficiently. Sewing weight cotton (50/3) was too thick and stiff for the edge. When I tried 30 weight/2-ply machine embroidery thread, I was pleasantly surprised. This thread is thicker than the fine embroidery threads, and more softly twisted. When stitched, the twist loosens and fills in the stitch with a fuller look. This thread is the one I prefer for this technique. Sulky rayon is another good choice if you like a shiny stitch.

Stitching

Prepare your machine by threading it with fine machine embroidery thread (60/2) in the bobbin and 30/2 machine embroidery thread on the top. Use a size

70 or 75 needle, and put the open-toe appliqué foot on the machine. Sew samples by placing a raw edge on top of another fabric and stitch along the raw edge. Adjust the stitch width and length to your preference, starting with #2 width and #2 length. Adjust tensions so that no bobbin thread is showing on the top of the work, and the top thread is locked properly. Loosen the top tension slightly to soften the stitch, if desired.

Straight lines and gentle curves are easy to stitch against, but tight corners and points can be tricky. Practice these before starting on your project. Review the pivoting techniques covered in the Satin Stitch unit in Chapter Five. When approaching a tight curve, you must pivot and control when the needle swings to the left. Try moving the width back to "0" in tight spots, taking it back to the predetermined width at the time you want the stitch to go to the left. When stitching inside and outside points, a stitch must be placed in the corner to stabilize the fabric. The illustrations below indicate proper placement of the stitches.

Techniques for this will be different for every computerized machine. Try different settings and adjustments until you have control over the stitch and can keep stitches evenly spaced throughout the piece.

To lock the stitches, make a few very short, straight stitches along the raw edge of the appliqué piece, then proceed with the piece or go on to the next piece. You can now cut out the backs, if you want. This reduces the layers you have to quilt through, but it is not necessary.

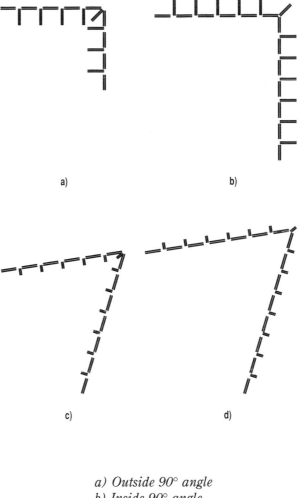

a) Outside 90° angle
b) Inside 90° angle
c) Outside 60° angle
d) Inside 60° angle

CHAPTER SIXTEEN

Broderie Perse Appliqué

Broderie perse is the technique of appliquéing chintz fabrics onto a background fabric. These chintz prints are cut out and arranged into a design on the base fabric. The appliqué can be made from one piece cut out, or from several cut out, which are rearranged and overlapped to create a collage effect.

The French words *broderie perse* mean "Persian embroidery." This technique was popular in America during the eighteenth century for bedcoverings. Traditionally, the cutouts were pasted onto a background fabric that was stretched in a frame. Once the paste was dry, the fabric was taken out of the frame, and the cutouts were stitched down with invisible stitches.

Photographs of antique chintz quilts, Baltimore Album quilts, and floral appliqué quilts are good sources of inspiration for the design process.

Most of the fabrics are printed in a repeat pattern, and the mirror image of the design is not available. This requires you to cut the design apart so that you can rotate, cut off, and rearrange individual parts to get the design to face opposite directions and give you the finished design you desire.

When working with the machine, the techniques must be adapted. The following ideas are only that—ideas. Experiment and see what other ways you can come up with to adapt traditional hand appliqué techniques, such as Hawaiian quilting, to your sewing machine.

Begin by preparing the chintz. The simplest method is to blanket stitch the raw edges.

1) Identify which chintz units are to be used. Use the techniques given in Chapter Fifteen to prepare the edges. If you choose Jeanne Hutchinson's method using fusing web, place the web across the print line and fuse. You will then be able to cut the chintz out exactly on the line. If working with Thread Fuse, stitch on this print line, and cut as close to it as possible. This will prevent any background color from appearing through the stitches.

2) Create the design you want by placing the chintz cutouts in position.

3) Press and fuse in place. Now you are ready to stitch.

TIP: When stitching the edges, consider changing the top thread color to match the fabric as it changes color. This has a beautiful blending effect, and the stitches become part of the fabric, instead of an outline or frame around the print.

If you want an invisible stitch around the chintz, use the Mock Hand appliqué techniques. Making the freezer paper patterns will be the tricky part, and before beginning, read Chapter Eleven on using a photocopy machine. I find it invaluable for broderie perse.

Method #1—Photocopied patterns

1) Place the chintz design, fabric right-side-up, on the photocopy machine and copy. This will produce a mirror image of the fabric.

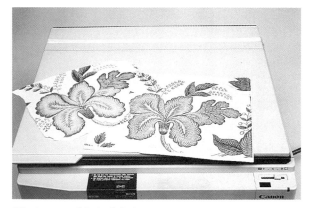

Photocopy chintz fabric

2) Lay a sheet of freezer paper, plastic-side-down, on top of the photocopy pattern. Carefully trace in the details that you want along the folded edge. This process will give you a pattern that duplicates the print edge of the chintz, instead of leaving a margin of background fabric that will show later.

Trace photocopy onto freezer paper

3) Cut the tracing out along the line.

Cut paper carefully

4) Position the freezer paper pattern on the wrong side of the chintz, aligning the edge of the paper to the print line of the design. Press.

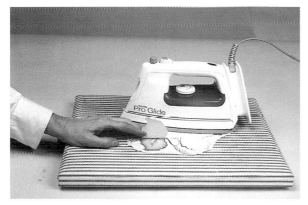

Press freezer paper onto chintz

5) Cut out each chintz design, leaving a ³⁄₁₆" seam allowance along all edges. Clip and trim as necessary (refer to Chapter Ten, page 68 if you need information).

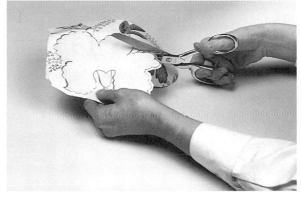

Cut seam allowance

6) Roll the edges over and glue them in place with a fresh glue stick. Check to be sure that the finished edge is along the print line of the fabric.

7) Design and position the cutouts onto the base fabric.

8) Stitch, following the instructions in Chapter Twelve. Cut away the parts of the background fabric underneath the chintz to remove the paper. This will also eliminate the bulk and make the quilting softer.

Method #2—Photocopying onto freezer paper

Having a photocopy machine available will save hours of tracing time. This method is basically the same as Method #1, except that the pattern is photocopied directly onto the freezer paper. This method is limited to chintz pieces the size of a sheet of paper, unless you want to work with pieces by overlapping and butting them.

Photocopy of fabric on freezer paper

1) Cut freezer paper into sheets the same size as the copier paper. Feed in each sheet manually, with the freezer paper plastic-side-down on top of a sheet of copier paper.

2) Place the chintz cutout right-side-up on the copier.

3) Manually feed the freezer paper/copier paper sandwich into the machine. The fabric design will be copied directly onto the freezer paper, eliminating the need to trace the copy onto the freezer paper.

4) Carefully cut the copy out on the print line and press onto wrong side of chintz, aligning edges exactly.

Freezer paper pressed onto fabric

5) Continue with steps 5 through 8 above.

For detailed information about broderie perse and other techniques used to create chintz quilts, try to obtain a copy of *Chintz Quilts: Unfading Glory* by Shiell and Bullard. This book will help you design your own quilt, using chintz prints. The beautiful decorator fabrics available today just might lure you into creating one of these beauties.

Keep Going

I hope by now you are dreaming up lots of ideas for using machine appliqué. It may be that you never liked appliqué much before now, except to look at someone else's work, and now you find that it is all you want to do. This seems to be a normal reaction my students have to these techniques. We call these methods "instant gratification."

Well, hold on, because we're not through yet. We're now going to go beyond traditional uses of appliqué patterns and designs and adapt the Mock Hand appliqué technique to other uses.

PART FOUR

Beyond Just Appliqué

CHAPTER SEVENTEEN

Curved Piecing à la Appliqué

How many of you just can't wait to start a curved piecing project? Few machine quilters enjoy the process of cutting out each unit with a template, clipping and pinning the two curved edges, lining them up under the foot, and hopefully sewing accurately enough that the curve turns out to be a curve! Besides this, the size of the block is limited to 2" or larger to even be able to work with it under the presser foot. What if we could make curved piecing easier than sewing a straight line?

Drunkard's Path and Curved Two Patch System Designs

This favorite quilt is a snap to make with this technique, as are any of the designs from the books *The Curved Two Patch System, Curves Unlimited,* and *Cutting Up with Curves* by Joyce Scholtzhauer. These books are excellent resources for designs and inspiration, and the grid can be any size you want.

Begin by making the templates the size you want. Draw two 4" squares on graph paper. Add ¼" seam allowance to one square, and glue the graph paper to cardboard, plastic, etc., to make a template. Example:

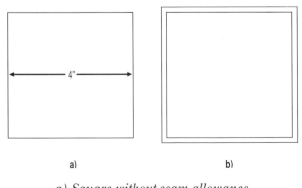

a) Square without seam allowance
b) Square with seam allowance

If your block needs to be 4" square (finished), cut this template 4 ½" square. Do not cut the concave (inside) curve from this square. Cut the number of fabric squares needed for your project.

On the second square, make two marks that are approximately three quarters the length of any two adjacent sides. This square does not have seam allowances added.

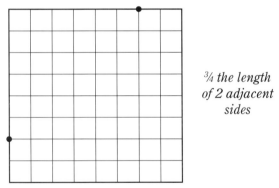

¾ the length of 2 adjacent sides

Using a compass, position the point at the corner. Place the pencil end of the compass on the mark on one side of the square. Draw to the mark on the adjacent side.

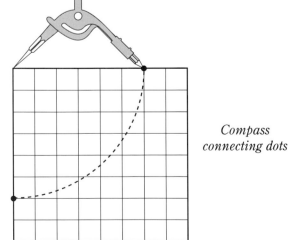

Compass connecting dots

Draw in ¼" seam allowances for the right-angle corner, but do not add a seam allowance to the curve. Make a template for this piece.

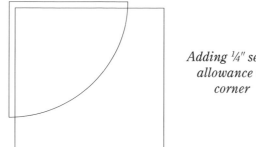

Adding ¼" seam allowance to corner

Trace the new pie-shaped template onto freezer paper, making one freezer paper pattern for every block needed. To speed this process, use the photocopier method discussed on page 83, if possible. You could also try cutting multiple layers of paper if you have good cutting skills. Cut out the freezer paper patterns, being careful to make the curved edge smooth.

Once the pie-shaped paper units are cut, press the freezer paper onto the wrong side of the desired fabrics. Keep the right-angle corner straight with the grainline of the fabric. This will put the curve on the bias.

Press pie-shaped templates onto fabric

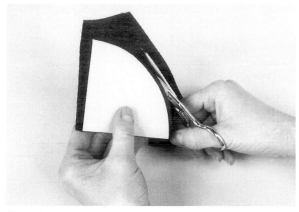

Cut seam allowance on curved edge

Cut out the shapes. When cutting, cut the fabric even with the freezer paper in the corner, but add a ³⁄₁₆" extension of fabric for seam allowance to the curve.

Using a fresh fabric-basting glue stick or the Quilter's GluTube, apply glue to the curved seam allowance. Also apply glue slightly onto the freezer paper. Carefully roll the seam allowance over to the freezer paper with small pinch-and-twist motions of your thumb and fingertip. (See page 70 for detailed instructions on gluing.) This is the trick: You can get a more precise curve from gluing than from stitching the seam!

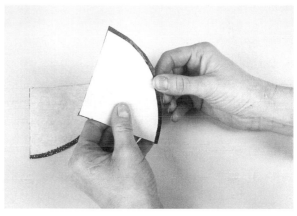

Glue seam allowance over edge

After all the curved edges are glued, you are ready to appliqué them to the squares. Position the pie-shaped piece on top of the square so that the corners align exactly. Pin into place.

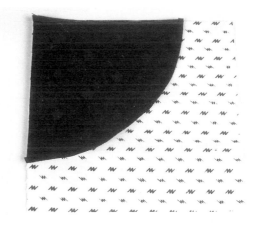

Position pie-shaped piece on square

With the machine set to do Mock Hand appliqué and using invisible thread (see page 86), stitch the curve onto the square. Be careful that the needle rubs the curve when stitching straight. You do not want to be able to see any of the stitching. These units can be chain sewn to save time and thread.

Stitch curve

After all the curves are stitched into place, turn the square over. Cut away the corner of the square, leaving a ¼" seam allowance beyond the stitching. (Keep these pieces; they are perfect for another project, in a smaller grid. The corner is already square. Just apply a smaller pie-shaped piece of freezer paper and repeat the process above.)

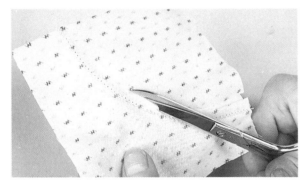

Trim curve on back side

If using a basting glue stick, dampen the curved seam allowance that was glued to dissolve the glue. If using the GluTube, no water is necessary. Gently pull the freezer paper out of this seam, and press from the wrong side. Assemble the blocks into any design or pattern you choose. The accuracy of this method is extremely high. Because all of the pie-shaped pieces were identical and were positioned the same, the distance from the curved seam end to the corners is always the same. This is not always the case when piecing a seam.

Clamshells

The clamshell pattern can be done with the same method used for Drunkard's Path. This pattern used to be considered for quilters with a great deal of experience, time, and patience. Now beginners will have perfect results, automatically!

Instead of viewing this as a patchwork pattern, let's turn it into an appliqué. It will be done more accurately as well as being stronger when finished.

Use a commercial pattern for the clamshell shape, or draft your own. To do this, simply choose the size clamshell you want and draw a circle, using a compass, with that diameter. Draw a line through the center of the circle, making sure that the line intersects with the hole from the compass.

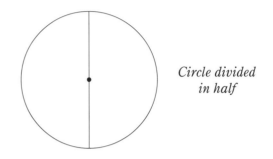

Circle divided in half

With a T-square or C-Thru® ruler, draw a line perpendicular to the first line.

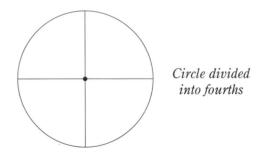

Circle divided into fourths

Draw lines that extend parallel to center lines in the bottom corners, extending from the edge of the circle.

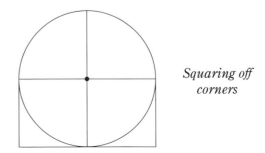

Squaring off corners

Place the point of the compass in these corners, one at a time, and draw in a curve that will cut the original circle at the half and bottom quarter points.

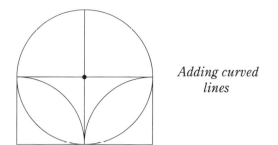

Adding curved lines

Before cutting out the shape, add ¼" seam allowances to the new curved lines. Do not add seam allowance to the outer curve at the top. This is your template. You can either use the template method with spray starch (see page 74 for instructions) or make individual freezer paper patterns, using a fabric-basting glue stick or GluTube.

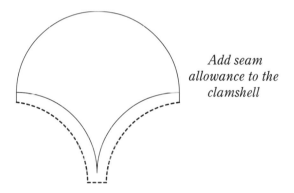

Add seam allowance to the clamshell

If using freezer paper patterns, you are now ready to trace this shape as many times as needed onto freezer paper (or use the copy machine). Cut out the freezer paper shapes, keeping the outer curve as accu-

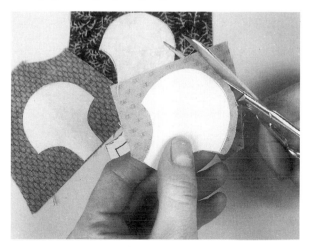

Cut out clamshell units

rate as possible. Press these paper pieces onto the wrong side of the desired fabric. Cut the shapes out of the fabric, cutting even with the freezer paper on the inside curves at the bottom, but cutting a ³⁄₁₆" extension of seam allowance on the upper, outside curve.

Using a glue stick, glue the outside curves over to the freezer paper, keeping them smooth. Do not clip these curves.

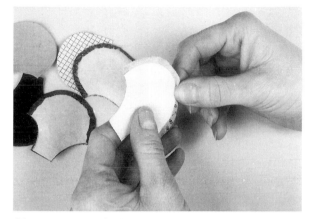

Glue over curved edge

After the raw edges have been glued over the paper, the shells are ready to be placed on the base fabric. Prepare your base fabric as follows: Placement begins from the top and works to the bottom. Lay the first horizontal row of shells in a straight line across the top of the base fabric. Stitch in place, using the Mock Hand appliqué stitch or blanket stitch, whichever look you prefer.

Stitch first row of shells

After the first row is stitched in place, remove the freezer paper, if it was used.

Remove freezer paper

Position the second row of shells, making sure that the top curve lines up with and covers the seam allowances of the first row. Pin in place and stitch as for the first row. Continue these steps until all the rows have been sewn in place and all the paper has been removed.

Position second row and pin

Templates

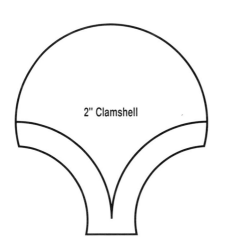

2" Clamshell

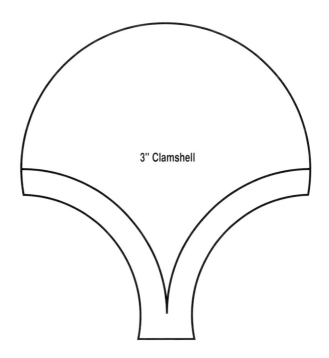

3" Clamshell

Templates

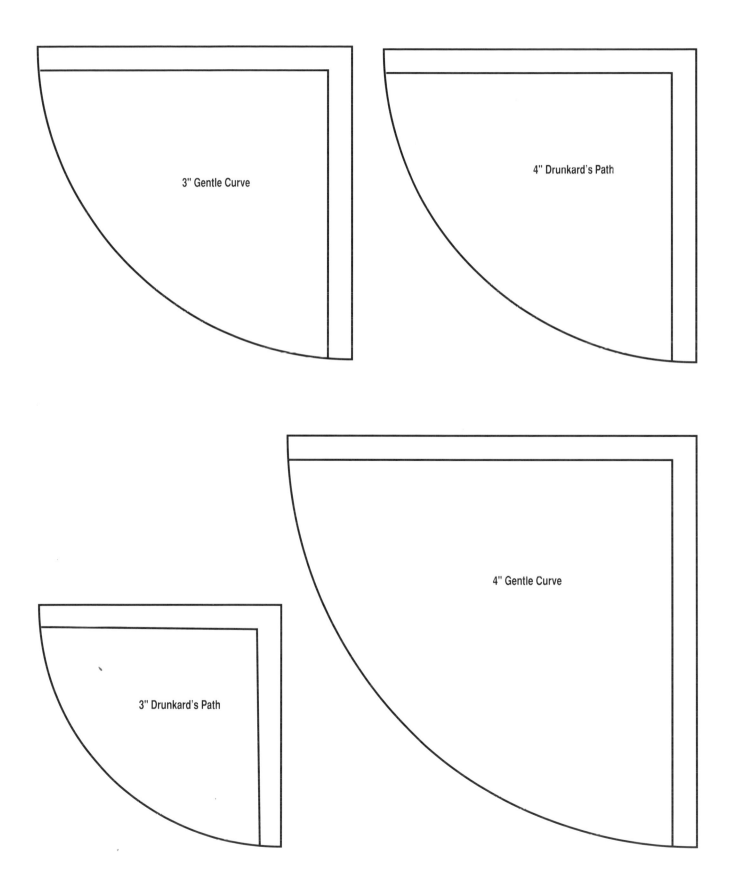

3" Gentle Curve

4" Drunkard's Path

3" Drunkard's Path

4" Gentle Curve

CHAPTER EIGHTEEN

Stained Glass Appliqué

Stained Glass appliqué has come and gone and come again in popularity with quilters. It is never totally out of fashion, but its popularity is inconsistent, as opposed to appliqué and pieced quilts.

The sewing machine and the blind stitch make creating a stained glass piece very easy. If you have never tried this form of appliqué, do so now. Today's vibrantly colored fabrics—cottons, lamé, satins, silks, etc.—produce truly luminescent "windows" of cloth.

Designs

You will find designs and patterns for stained glass from many sources. The most appropriate designs come from patterns for actual stained glass. These can be purchased from a stained glass store. To meet your needs, they can be reduced or enlarged with a photocopy machine.

Copy the original pattern onto freezer paper. This tracing will be cut up into individual units for a cutting pattern. Trace the pieces onto the paper side of the freezer paper. Do not add seam allowances. The pieces will be cut on the design line and the raw edges butted snugly to one another, like a jigsaw puzzle. You will not need to do reverse image tracings because the paper will be applied to the right side of the fabric. Number the pieces for easy identification when ready to lay out the design. Carefully cut the units apart. Leave the original pattern intact; it will be used for the layout.

Fabrics

The fabrics will be easier to work with if they are backed with an iron-on interfacing or a fusing web, as described in Chapter Two. These products stabilize the edges of the fabrics and add body to the piece for hanging. If the piece is to be used as a bed quilt instead of a wall hanging, use a very soft interfacing, or spray starch the fabrics three times to give the fabric extra body. Choose which method you want to use on your fabrics and prepare them in this manner.

Press the freezer paper pattern units onto the right side of the fabrics. Carefully cut along the edge of the paper. Cut each piece accurately so that the pieces of the design fit back together tightly. After cutting out the units, prepare the base fabric by pressing in centering lines. Lay the fabric on top of the original pattern and center. Pin the two together.

TIP: If your base fabric is dark or if you have problems seeing through it, the use of a light box or other light source is indispensable.

Bias Strips for Lead Lines

You can either use purchased bias tape, or make your own. Purchased tape is easier, but color selection and quality might be poor. Making your own bias gives you more flexibility in color and fabric selection and is not that time-consuming.

The lead lines for Stained Glass appliqué should be ¼" or smaller. Be sure that the strips are true bias, because tight curves require the stretching ability of bias. Refer to Chapter Ten, pages 77 through 81 for making perfect bias for this technique.

After all the appliqué pieces are prepared, you are ready to build the design onto the background fabric. It is very helpful to use a light box for this process. I do not recommend drawing the placement lines onto the background fabric: Through the cutting and preparation stages, the pattern pieces are apt to change shape slightly and probably won't match the drawn lines exactly. The light box allows you to place the fabric on top of the pattern and see through the fabric for placement.

Prepare the background fabric by folding it into fourths and pressing in registration lines. If your pattern is in sections, you might want to prepare a full-scale layout of the finished design to use for placement. Mark the centering registration lines on the pattern to be used to line up with the background fabric.

Assembling

Position the background fabric over the layout pattern, matching the registration lines, and tape or pin in place. Examine the original pattern to see if there are any "lead lines" placed in the background, such as squares or diagonals to create a grid effect behind the colored "glass." If there are, these pieces of bias must be placed and stitched first.

Position the pattern units onto the base fabric, aligning the edges for a tight fit. If you are using a fusible web such as Wonder-Under, peel off the paper backing before positioning it onto the base fabric, then press into place. Work carefully to prevent the base fabric from shifting. If you are working with interfaced or starched fabric, apply fabric-basting glue stick to the edges to secure them. Once the "glass" pieces are placed and secured, you can begin to place the bias. This can either be pinned or glued to hold in place.

Before applying the bias to the piece, examine where short pieces will be used and where long pieces will run continuously. The short pieces should be applied first and stitched in place. Their raw ends will then be covered by the longer pieces. Work from the back of the design to the front. This will help you identify which pieces should be worked first. Attach the bias with pins, glue stick, or basting. Take the time to ease accurately around difficult curves and points.

TIP: Bias can be formed into curves and shapes at the ironing board with a steam iron. Lay the bias in the shape desired, and set the shape with steam. The bias will assume and keep this shape as you position it onto the project.

Stitching

Set your machine to do a small zigzag stitch. Use 60 weight/2-ply black (or matching color) machine embroidery thread or smoke invisible nylon. Put the open-toe appliqué foot or the edge stitch foot on the machine. Use a size 70 needle. Stitch both sides of the tape, letting the swing of the needle go just off the edge of the tape onto the "glass" fabric. This tiny stitch gives a hand stitched appearance to your work.

TIP: To prevent distortion, work with a pin or stiletto in your hand to help ease the tape under the foot.

After all the bias is stitched into place, finish the piece by quilting, bordering, binding, or framing.

Reverse Appliqué Stained Glass
by Cathy Robiscoe

Cathy Robiscoe, a quilter from Bozeman, Montana, developed an extraordinary new technique for Stained Glass appliqué using reverse appliqué techniques and freezer paper. Cathy shared this method with shopowners at the October 1991 Houston Quilt Market. Below is a brief explanation of her technique. Cathy has designed a line of Stained Glass patterns which include very detailed instructions for her technique. (See suppliers listing for address.)

If using one of Cathy's patterns, you will find that the lead lines are ¼" wide, instead of the standard single line. If you are using a standard stained glass pattern, use a double pencil, like those used to draw ¼" lines around piecing templates, to trace over the lines to create the ¼" lead line. Keep the single original line in the center, between the new lines being traced.

Retrace lines with double pencil

Use a piece of freezer paper larger than the pattern. If working with a large pattern, glue the edges of two pieces together, if necesary. The paper needs to be in one piece.

Trace the stained glass pattern onto the freezer paper. Check to see if reverse image drawing is necessary. Trace each of the double lines ¼" apart. These will be the "lead" of the finished piece.

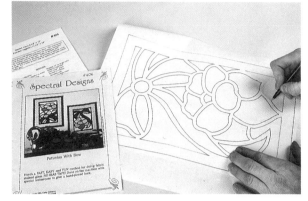

Trace pattern onto freezer paper

Lay the freezer paper onto your rotary cutter mat, and with a single blade art knife, carefully cut along each line. You will be cutting out the area where the colored "glass" will be showing. The paper left is the "lead" lines.

Cut away inner areas

Press freezer paper onto black fabric

After all the units are cut and removed, carefully lay the freezer paper pattern onto a piece of solid black (or color of your choice) fabric, and press to secure the freezer paper to the fabric.

Working only a few sections at a time in a small area, carefully cut the black fabric ³⁄₁₆" from the freezer paper. Clip any inside curves halfway to the paper, and clip any corners up to one thread from the paper.

Cut away excess black and clip where necessary

Using the Quilter's GluTube, apply glue to the seam allowance and the freezer paper. Let dry, then gently roll the seam allowance over onto the paper. Work on a flat surface when doing this to prevent distorting the pattern. Cathy recommends using a round toothpick to help manipulate the seam allowance.

Glue and roll edges over

Once you have a few sections prepared, carefully turn the black over, and place the desired color under one of the openings. Dabbing a few spots of glue on the paper back will help secure the colored "glass" in place while stitching.

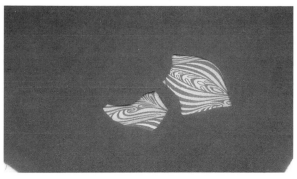

Position colored "glass"

Using a small zigzag stitch, stitch around the opening with 60/2 black machine embroidery thread. Position the needle to just rub the black folded edge, but stitch in the "glass" when the needle is in the left swing. This will give a hand-stitched appearance.

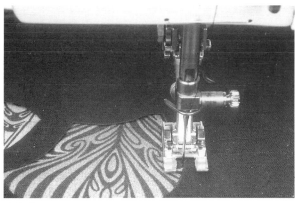

Stitch

When stitching, carefully pivot around curves and secure points as discussed in Chapter Twelve.

Once the area is stitched, turn the piece over and carefully trim the excess fabric 1/8"–3/16" from the stitching.

Trim away excess

Continue cutting out additional black areas and adding the colored "glass" in the same manner. The finished product is neat, accurate and beautiful.

Reverse appliqué techniques can be adapted to many uses other than Stained Glass. Let your imagination and creativity carry you away.

Cathedral Window

have included this technique here because it uses Mock Hand appliqué techniques and can be done totally on the machine in a fraction of the time required by hand. Directions given are for a 12" pillow top. (Credit is given to The Quilted Apple in Phoenix, Arizona, for the border technique used here). The pattern is based on a folding technique and produces a quilt that has no seam allowances, no batting, and no backing fabric. It is self-contained. At the last step, it is automatically quilted.

The technique uses two basic elements, the backing squares and the window squares. Take extra care to straighten the fabric of the backing squares so that the grainlines are perpendicular to each other. Off-grain squares will not lie or turn properly, causing many problems in all steps.

These instructions use 9" squares of backing fabric, but you can make the squares any size you desire, remembering that the folding technique reduces the backing squares to one-fourth of their original size. It will take four folded squares to take up the space of one unfolded square.

Cut four 9" squares of muslin or chosen background fabric. Fold each muslin square in half, and sew ¼" seams on each end. These can be chain sewn to save time.

Open the pocket and position so that the seams are matched, one on the other. Start sewing at the end (backstitch) and continue across the seams about 1". Backstitch, leave a 2" opening unstitched, backstitch again, and complete seam, backstitching at end.

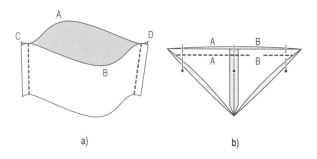

a)

b)

a) Open the pocket
b) Stitch raw edges together, leaving an opening

Turn right-side-out, using a point turner to make the points very clean. *Very carefully press,* keeping sides straight and square. Press the opening closed neatly (this can be hand stitched closed, but is not necessary)

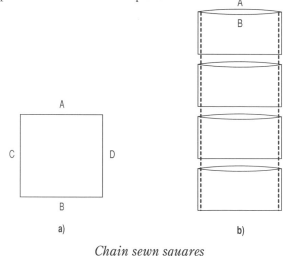

a)

b)

Chain sewn squares

Turn right side out—close opening

Carefully fold the points into the center. Finger press and pin, then steam press. The new corners need to be very accurate.

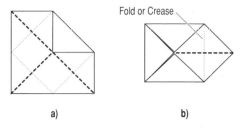

a) Press points to center b) Show crease when unfolded

After the four squares are pressed, place two of them together, matching corners, and press lines. Stitch along the press line, backstitching at the beginning and end.

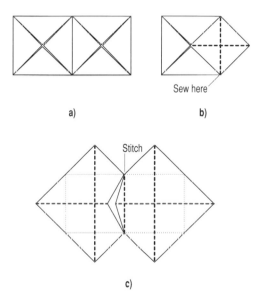

a) Position two squares side by side
b) Take two adjacent flaps and stitch together
c) Squares joined and flat again

Repeat this process with the other two squares. Join the two pairs together in the same manner.

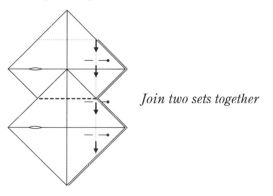

Join two sets together

Cut four 13" x 5" strips of fabric for the border. Fold each of the four strips in half lengthwise. Press, unfold, and fold in half crosswise. Mark the center point of each strip with a pin.

Border strip—folded in half and creased

Unfold the strips. Lay one flat on the table, right-side-up. Lay the wrong side of the joined squares on top of the border strip, with the centers of each matching. Place the pressed crease lines of the open triangular flaps directly on top of the pressed line of the border strip. Machine stitch on top of the crease line of the flaps. Do not turn the corners.

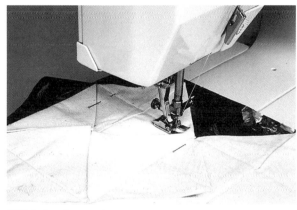

Stitch borders onto squares

Stitch the remaining borders onto the squares in the same manner. Fold the triangular flaps down onto the squares. Position the points of the flaps in the center of each square, and secure with pins. Anchor the points by placing three stitches into each point. Do this by placing the needle in the very center, then stitching forward three stitches, backstitching three stitches, and stitching forward again six stitches. You can also do this by setting your machine on 3-step zigzag and changing the needle position to the right. Insert the needle where the points meet, needle in right swing. The needle will make three stitches to the left and back again. Pivot the fabric and repeat for the other side, or change the needle position to the left. Repeat for all flaps. These stitches produce neat and secure points.

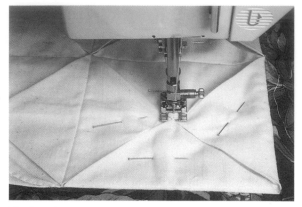

Tack points to center

Miter the border corners by folding the block diagonally from corner to corner. Pin borders together. With a marker and a straight edge, extend the diagonal line of the pillow across the border. This should be a 45° angle and marks the stitching line. Machine stitch, starting at the inside corner. Trim excess fabric and press open.

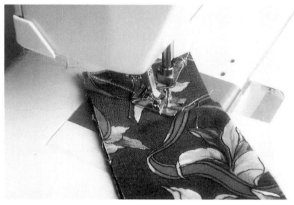

a) Stitch corner to miter

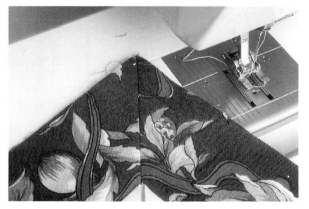

b) Finished

The next step is to place the windows. Cut four 2 ⅝" squares of the print you have chosen. Place them, one at a time, over each of the seams joining the backing squares. Pin in place.

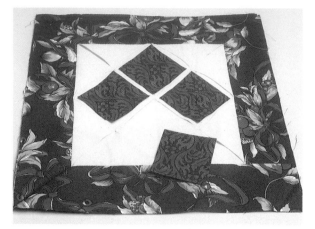

Place windows

Carefully roll the unstitched, folded edge of the backing square over the raw edge of the window square. Fold the edge back until the fold extends from corner to corner. Repeat for each window and pin each edge in place.

Roll edge over windows and pin

Starting in one corner, fold back the edge and stitch down, using a straight stitch or the Mock Hand appliqué stitch. Keep very close to the edge as with appliqué, beginning and ending at the corners. Keep the needle in the corner and prepare to stitch the next folded edge.

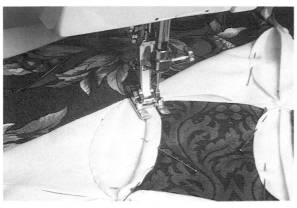

Stitch edges

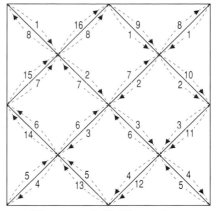

Diagram of stitching order

Continue this process until you come to the opposite corner. Pivot the block and repeat for the other side of this row. Stitch the other diagonal line, corner to corner, then stitch the remaining folds in the same manner.

Once the folds are stitched, add ruffles or welting to the outside edges of the border to finish the pillow top. If you decide to do a quilt of Cathedral Window, sew the folds in diagonal rows. This will eliminate turning the quilt to sew around the squares.

Conclusion

I sincerely hope that this book has opened new horizons for you. I also hope it has given you the feeling that appliqué is approachable, fun, and beautiful without being time-consuming. Many of my students called appliqué the "A" word before taking this class, and then later wrote to me (with pictures enclosed) about all the wonderful appliqué they were doing—and loving it.

Don't stop here. Your sewing machine is a valuable tool, and with you, it can create marvelous works of art, equal to anyone's hand work. You just need to experiment, learn as much as you can about *your* machine, and adventure beyond what has already been done. Above all else, ENJOY the process.

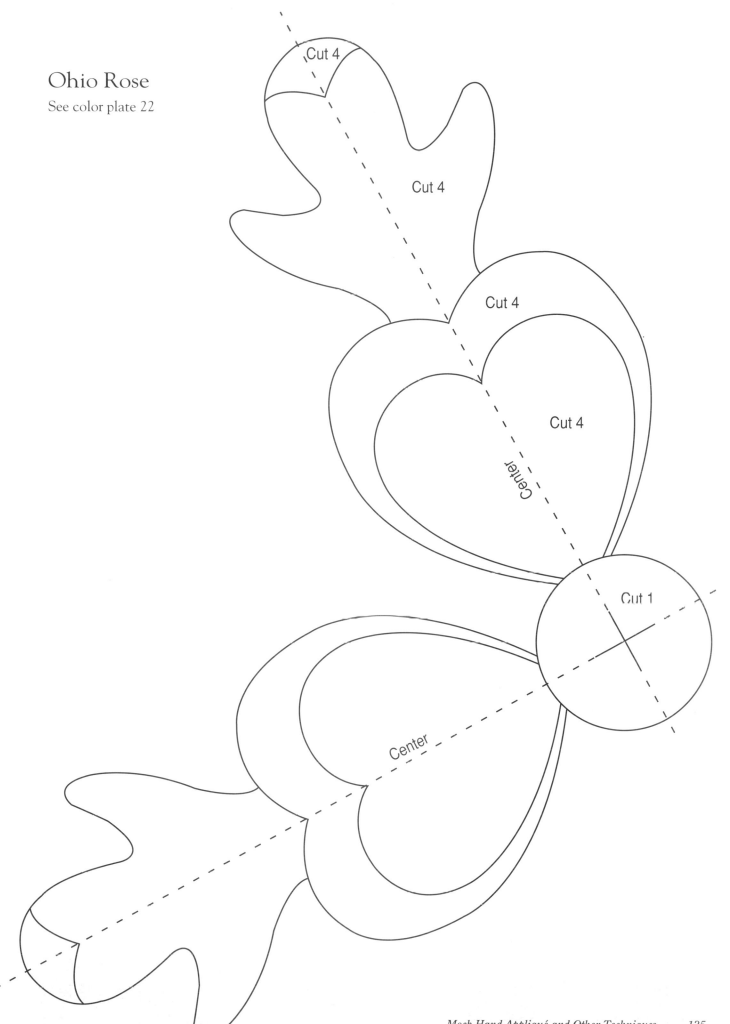

Ohio Rose

See color plate 22

Cut 4

Cut 4

Cut 4

Cut 4

Cut 4

Cut 1

Center

Center

Lancaster Rose

See color plate 17

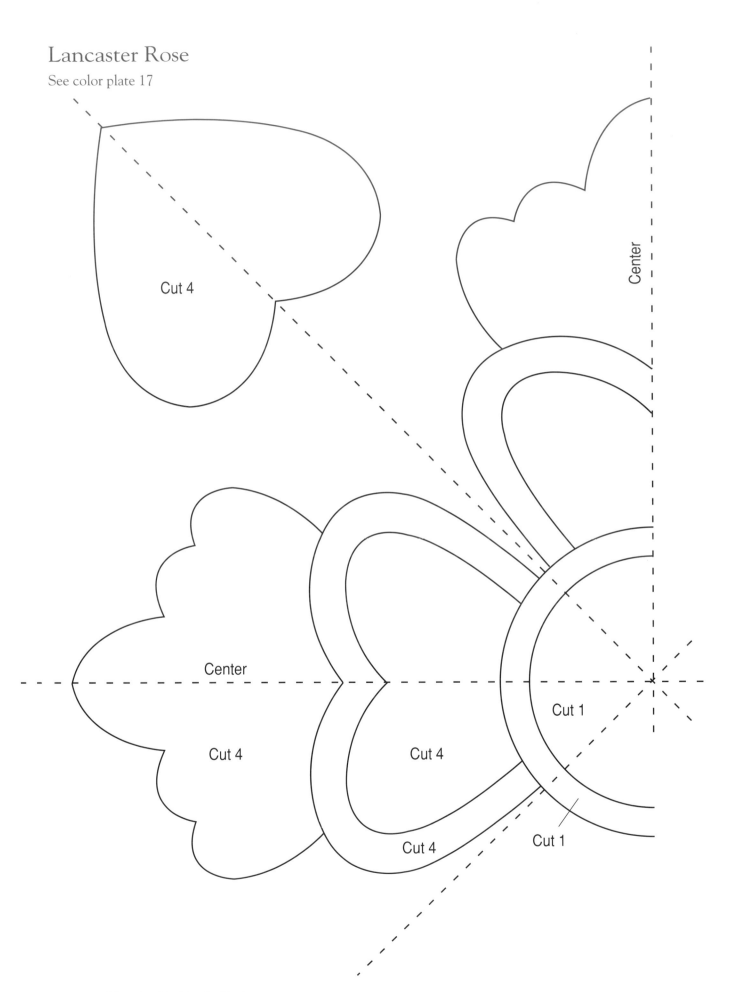

Cut 4

Center

Cut 4

Center

Cut 4

Cut 1

Cut 4

Cut 1

Source List

Most of the supplies listed in this book can be obtained from your local quilt shop or sewing machine dealer. If you have trouble finding any of the required materials, they can be mail ordered directly from Harriet at:

Harriet's Treadle Arts
6390 West 44th Avenue
Wheat Ridge, CO 80033
(303) 424-2742

Stained glass patterns from Cathy Robiscoe can be ordered from:

Spectral Designs
P.O. Box 4020
Bozeman, MT 59772

Shopowners should be able to obtain all needed supplies from wholesale distributors. Specific distributors will be furnished upon request. Harriet's Treadle Arts does not wholesale products.

PATTERN COMPANIES

Hickory Hollow
235 N. Main St.
Versailles, KY 40383

Jo Sonja's Folk Art Studio
P.O. Box 9080, 2136 Third St.
Eureka, CA 95501

The Critter Pattern Works
204 Independence Ct.
Blandon, PA 19510

Piecemakers
1720 Adams Avenue
Costa Mesa, CA 92626

Donna's Designs
702 West Arch Street
Searcy, AR 72143

The Stitch Connection
43601 Gatehouse Ct.
Canton, MI 48187

Little Quilts
4828 Hampton Lake Drive
Marietta, GA 30068

Fabricraft
P.O. Box 962
Cardiff by the Sea, CA 92007

Bibliography

Cory, Pepper. *Happy Trails*. Lafayette, Ca.: C & T Publishing, 1991.

Develin, Nancy. *Guide To Machine Quilting*.   Glen Burnie, Md.: Starshine Stitchery Press, 1976.

Hall, Carrie A. and Kretsinger, Rose G. *The Romance of the Patchwork Quilt in America*. New York: Bonanza Books, 1935.

Kretsinger, Rose G. "Old Time Quilting: Oriental Poppy." *Quilter's Newsletter Magazine*, April 1980, page 31.

Lee, Barbara. *Successful Machine Appliqué*. Atlanta: Yours Truly, Inc., 1978.

McKelvey, Susan. *Scrolls & Banners to Trace*. Millersville, Md.: Wallflower Designs, 1990.

My Bernina Guide. Steckborn, Switzerland: Fritz Gegauf Ltd., 1990.

Reeder, Gail S. *Creative Appliqué*. Norcross, Ga.: Willcraft Publishers, 1896.

Schlotzhauer, Joyce. *The Curved Two-Patch System*. McLean, Va.: EPM Publications, Inc., 1982.

Sienkiewicz, Elly. *Baltimore Beauties and Beyond, Vol. I*. Lafayette, Ca.: C & T Publishing, 1989.

Technical Advice for Sewing Textiles. Herzogenrath, Germany: Ferd. Schmetz GmbH.

Index

About the Author

Harriet Hargrave has been teaching machine arts since 1976, and her affinity for sewing machines and their capabilities continues. As a quilt shop owner and as a teacher, she has many opportunities to share her knowledge and skill. She has been teaching throughout the United States since 1985, and she has also taught in England, Ireland, Canada, Hawaii, Australia, and New Zealand.

Harriet's interest in machine arts began in the early 1970's when she attended a demonstration given by a sewing machine company educator. She was amazed to watch the machine create magic with thread and an electric needle, in a fraction of the time similar results could be achieved by hand. Needle painting became an obsession, and through a lot of experimentation, Harriet mastered her skills in machine needle arts. This culminated in the development of machine quilting, for which Harriet is internationally known.

Harriet has a degree in Textiles and Clothing from Colorado State University. She owns and operates Harriet's Treadle Arts in Wheat Ridge, Colorado, with her mother, Frances Frazier. She resides in Arvada, Colorado, with her teenage daughter Carrie.

Other Fine Quilting Books
From C & T Publishing

❧

An Amish Adventure, Roberta Horton

Appliqué 12 Easy Ways!, Elly Sienkiewicz

Baltimore Album Quilts, Historic Notes and Antique Patterns, Elly Sienkiewicz

Baltimore Beauties and Beyond (2 Volumes), Elly Sienkiewicz

Boston Commons Quilt, Blanche Young and Helen Young Frost

Calico and Beyond, Roberta Horton

A Celebration of Hearts, Jean Wells and Marina Anderson

Crazy Quilt Handbook, Judith Montano

Crazy Quilt Odyssey, Judith Montano

Crosspatch, Pepper Cory

Fans, Jean Wells

Fine Feathers, Marianne Fons

Flying Geese Quilt, Blanche Young and Helen Young Frost

Friendship's Offering, Susan McKelvey

Happy Trails, Pepper Cory

Heirloom Machine Quilting, Harriet Hargrave

Irish Chain Quilt, Blanche Young and Helen Young Frost

Landscapes & Illusions, Joen Wolfrom

Let's Make Waves, Marianne Fons and Liz Porter

Light and Shadows, Susan McKelvey

Mandala, Katie Pasquini

Mariner's Compass, Judy Mathieson

Memorabilia Quilting, Jean Wells

New Lone Star Handbook, Blanche Young and Helen Young Frost

Perfect Pineapples, Jane Hall and Dixie Haywood

Picture This, Jean Wells and Marina Anderson

Plaids and Stripes, Roberta Horton

PQME Series: Milky Way Quilt, Jean Wells

PQME Series: Nine-Patch Quilt, Jean Wells

PQME Series: Pinwheel Quilt, Jean Wells

PQME Series: Stars & Hearts Quilt, Jean Wells

Quilting Designs from Antique Quilts, Pepper Cory

Quilting Designs from the Amish, Pepper Cory

Story Quilts, Mary Mashuta

Trip Around the World Quilts, Blanche Young and Helen Young Frost

Visions: Quilts of a New Decade, Quilt San Diego

Working in Miniature, Becky Schaefer

Wearable Art for Real People, Mary Mashuta

3 Dimensional Design, Katie Pasquini

For more information write for a free catalog from

C & T Publishing
P.O. Box 1456
Lafayette, CA 94549
(1-800-284-1114)

TWO BOOKS IN ONE! Everything you always wanted to know about machine appliqué in Satin Stitch AND Mock Hand techniques.

The queen of machine arts and author of best-selling *Heirloom Machine Quilting*, Harriet Hargrave brings her well-known expertise and easy-to-learn techniques to anyone anxious to Satin Stitch clothing, accessories and quilts or to apply invisible machine stitching to favorite appliqué patterns. Learn the basics of Satin Stitch in the first book, then flip the book over for Mock Hand and other favorite techniques, including straight stitch, blanket stitch, broderie perse, curved piecing, cathedral windows, and stained glass. Each of the two books is self contained so that you can focus on the techniques you wish to learn and locate the information easily.

With Harriet's knowledge of equipment, supplies and stitching techniques, plus the inspirational color samples, this book will revolutionize your thinking about appliqué, and turn your dreams of appliqué masterpieces into reality.

- Copious illustrations
- Over 200 black and white photos
- 46 Color plates
- Patterns and index

"Harriet's first book was a watershed for machine quilting. Now she's done the same for machine appliqué. This is a craftswoman who understands how subtleties affect the outcome—thread, needle, fiber content, precision. But best of all, in *Mastering Machine Appliqué*, she's shared every bit of that knowledge in clear language and illustrations. Applause! Applause!"

—Robbie Fanning
Co-author, *The Complete Book of Machine Quilting*, Chilton Book Company
Co-author, *The Complete Book of Machine Embroidery*, Chilton Book Company

"Superb! An instant best-seller! She's done it again! Harriet Hargrave has written the one book for anyone seeking a really thorough step-by-step guide to creating beautiful appliqué on the machine. Packed with illustrative photos and presented in a straightforward, easy to follow format, *Mastering Machine Appliqué* is certain to become the authoritative text on the subject. Harriet deserves both praise and gratitude for this major contribution to the quilting world."

—Jan Burns, Editor, *Creative Quilting*

"Harriet inspires and delights the seamstress with beautiful designs and wonderful samples throughout the book. Whether the reader chooses to do traditional Satin Stitch appliqué or experiment with Mock Hand techniques, she will have no difficulty following the clear step-by-step instructions and photos. This book is really two-in-one!"

—JoAnn Pugh,
Marketing Manager–Software, Bernina of America

"Wow! A quick learn on state-of-the-art appliqué and sewing. Rather earth-shaking information on the miracles of modern sewing notions and machine techniques that revolutionizes the creative possibilities for both the hand and the machine appliqué lover. Harriet is a genius and teaches us so simply.

This book leaves me charged—I want to Mock Hand appliqué a vine border and center medallion wreath for my Baltimore Album Quilt then bring these to bloom, fashioning dimensional flowers by hand."

—Elly Sienkiewicz
Author of *Appliqué 12 Easy Ways!*, The *Baltimore Beauties* series on Baltimore Album Quilts, and *Dimensional Appliqué—Baskets, Blooms, and Baltimore Borders*

Mastering Machine Appliqué

The Satin Stitch

by Harriet Hargrave

C&T PUBLISHING

Photographs by Brian Birlauf, Denver, Colorado, unless otherwise noted

Editorial direction by Diane Pedersen, C & T Publishing

Copy editing by Jane Parkinson, Danville, California

Technical information edited by Janet Macik Myers, Fairfield, California

Book design and production coordination by Rose Sheifer Graphic Productions, Walnut Creek, California

Electronic Illustrations by Craig Diskowski, Edge Design, Cupertino, California

Copyright© 1991 Harriet Jane Hargrave

Published by C & T Publishing
P.O. Box 1456
Lafayette, California 94549

ISBN: 0-914881-45-0

Library of Congress Cataloging-in-Publication Data

Hargrave, Harriet.
    Mastering machine appliqué : mock hand appliqué and other techniques / by Harriet
Hargrave.. — 1st ed.
        p.   cm.
    Includes bibliographical references.
    ISBN 0-914881-45-0
    1. Machine appliqué.   I. Title.
TT779.H36   1991
746.44'5—dc20   91-58593
                                                                                       CIP

First Edition
First Printing
Printed in the United States of America

Tropical Fish by Debora Konchinsky. Many decorative stitches were added to regular Satin Stitch for texture and detail.

Christmas Treeskirt by Kathy Nicklas. Small details and outlines are created by Satin Stitch appliqué. The pattern used was Santa's Helper by Fabricraft.

Table of Contents

Acknowledgments

When someone asks how you developed a technique, it would be both untrue and unfair to answer that you did it by yourself. Every student of mine who has devised a new way to achieve the same end has altered the way I approach and teach the techniques in this book. So, a heartfelt thank you to all the innovative quilters and machine artists who have continually influenced my work over the past 17 years.

A special thank you to Diane Pedersen of C&T, who is always challenging me to rethink my ideas and who is totally supportive of my efforts to create the best book possible.

Thank you to Patty Albin, Nancy Barrett, Sharon Binder, Barbara Blum, Sharon Craig, Mary Devane, Barbara Eikmeier, Phyllis Freerksen, Gail Garber, Sandy Jones, Debora Konchinsky, Cynthia Kraft, Linda Mann, Donna Fite McConnell, Mace McEligot, Kathy Nicklas, Kathy Perry, Cathy Robiscoe, Sue Rasmussen, Arlene Stamper, Bev Tischhauser, and Barbara Trumbo for all their support and their untold hours behind the sewing machines to help produce the samples and projects in this book.

And most importantly, a special thank you to my mother and daughter for their unending patience in my quest to teach high quality machine arts. Without their support, none of this would be possible.

Dedication

Dedicated to my daughter Carrie, who has given up so much for me to be able to pursue my life's goals. Living with a traveling mother has not been easy, and she has steadfastly supported me in doing what makes me happy. In return, I hope that I have given her the permission to follow her dreams, for nothing is out of reach if you want it badly enough.

Introduction

Machine appliqué does not have a long, romantic history of genteel ladies stitching works of art. Instead, most popular forms of machine appliqué have been in existence only since the development of the zigzag sewing machine (many of the techniques in this book have been developed within the last two to five years). The popularity of machine appliqué has not been constant, and the quality has generally been moderate.

In 1978 I discovered a copy of *Successful Machine Appliqué* by Barbara Lee, and its excellent instructions greatly improved the look of my appliqué. With experience in machine embroidery, I found that by being particular about which supplies I used (especially threads), my appliqué took on a very neat, professional look. *Successful Machine Appliqué* went out of print several years ago, and there has not been a comprehensive handbook to replace it. This was my objective in writing *Mastering Machine Appliqué*. I also wanted to reinforce how wonderful a tool the sewing machine is, and how beautifully it can perform when you have good instructions and a careful selection of supplies.

Mastering Machine Appliqué is written for the person who has never done machine appliqué, as well as for the person who has mastered her machine, but wants to explore supplies, techniques, and ideas that will enhance her work. Whether you are a quilter, dressmaker, crafter, or just curious, there is something here for you.

Machine appliqué is one of the most versatile and rewarding of the machine arts. It can be used on clothing, home decorating items, quilts, crafts, and whatever else you can think of.

Both sections of this book contain invaluable information on sewing machines that will help you master your machine and make it perform to your liking. Once you feel comfortable with adjustments and parts, I hope you will explore all the fantastic things your machine will do for you.

How to Use This Book

෫

Specific brand names of supplies are given where possible because I have found over the years that these brands produce the most beautiful results. Similar products can often be found under different brand names, but they may not perform as well. If you are unable to find these exact products, experiment with what is available. If you are not happy with the results, continue searching for the recommended brand names. You will quickly discover that there is a vast difference between different brands of the same type of product.

If clothing and sewing are your main interests, you will be interested in the Satin Stitch techniques with the heavy stitching for their durability and beauty in defining the design. If you lean more toward quilting, the Mock Hand techniques help you create beautiful appliqués that not only look exactly like hand appliqué, but are more durable. You will find tried-and-true patterns such as Drunkard's Path, using curved piecing. Cathedral Window and Clamshells can be done on the machine in a fraction of the time of hand work, but with the look of hand stitching.

Satin Stitch and Mock Hand techniques are totally different. Thus, this book has been divided into two distinct books for ease in use. The first side gives complete information about achieving perfect satin stitching. Flip the book over, and the other side contains complete information on machine techniques that produce hand work effects. You will also find many valuable timesaving ideas. Each side is self-contained, but the detailed information in each book is a valuable reference. However, if you have never machine appliquéd before, I would suggest that you work through the Satin Stitch techniques first. These will teach you a great deal about your machine and how it works, as well as providing fabric manipulation skills.

Scan through all the information and become familiar with the terminology and techniques before attempting to do the actual stitching. This will give you a feel for where the information is and will allow you to gather all needed supplies before beginning. This book strives to recreate the atmosphere of a classroom: it starts with an explanation of the process, followed by step-by-step instructions for practicing the techniques, and finally, how to approach your first project.

PART ONE

Satin Stitch Appliqué

CHAPTER ONE

Equipment

atin Stitch appliqué requires specific equipment and supplies to obtain professional-looking results. You may already have many of these; others will be new products that you may have never heard of or used before. Read through the Equipment and Supplies chapters before starting any projects. Then you will be able to assemble everything before the project is started, and you will have a thorough understanding of the items and their use.

Sewing Machine

A zigzag machine is necessary for machine appliqué. It should have the ability to adjust stitch width and length while you sew. Directions given in this book are for machines that have a center needle position during basic sewing functions. Machines with a permanent left-hand needle position make it very difficult to accomplish these techniques. The quality of your equipment affects the quality of your work. A machine that has constant tension problems, gets hot after sewing for a period of time, has limited stitch capabilities, or won't sew well using different threads on top and bottom is going to give you poor results. Good quality equipment gives you good quality work. As you learn new decorative art skills, you may outgrow your equipment and want to purchase a new machine.

Suggested machine features:

1) Perfect tension adjustment, regardless of what combination of threads is put into the machine.

2) The ability to adjust the bobbin tension (with the bobbin case itself or by purchasing a separate bobbin case).

3) Up-and-down needle position on command.

(My machine allows me to do this with the foot control. One tap puts the needle down into the fabric, another tap brings it up to the highest position without my having to remove my hands from the project. This is a real help for control.)

4) Total stitch width adjustability. Many newer machines have push-button width control buttons that increase and decrease in .5 increments. This does not allow the stitch to be tapered smoothly and evenly when satin stitching. Lower-priced machines often only have three or four stitch width settings. Again, this precludes performing the machine techniques in this book. Check this feature on your machine before starting, and definitely check it when shopping for new equipment. The ultimate is a machine with unlimited stitch width settings on a dial that can be very finely adjusted while sewing.

5) The ability to sew for hours at high speed without overheating.

6) A reputable dealer who will help with minor adjustments and have an understanding of what you are doing.

The work surface around your machine is also important. A flat surface at the same level as the needle plate of the machine makes manipulation of the appliqué pieces easier. Otherwise, the fabric is constantly falling off the open arm or small machine surface. If your machine has a sewing table or extension plate that came with it, use it. If not, create one from wood or other material that can be cut in the shape of the open arm, attaching legs to make it the same height as the machine. This frees your hands to manipulate the shapes and sew accurately instead of fighting the fabric as it falls off the edge and gets caught on the machine. The following photo is a suggested working surface.

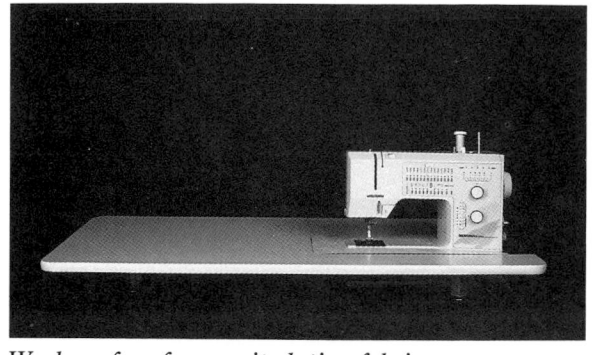

Work surface for manipulating fabric

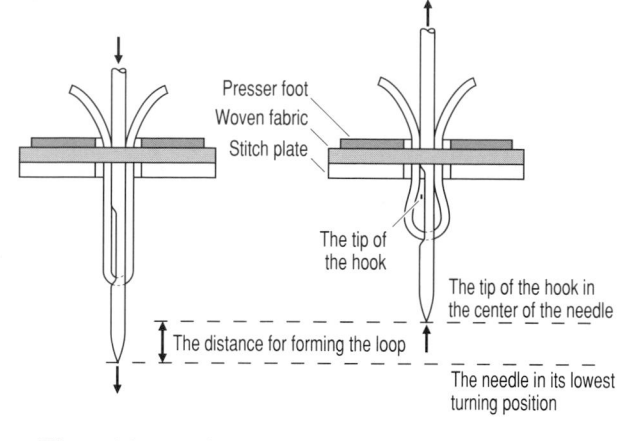

Presser foot
Woven fabric
Stitch plate

The tip of
the hook

The tip of the hook in
the center of the needle

The distance for forming the loop

The needle in its lowest
turning position

Thread loop being formed as needle leaves fabric

Sewing Machine Needles

Needles are critical in obtaining a smooth, even stitch, especially when satin stitching. The extreme density of the stitches tends to dull and heat a needle. You will need to change the needle more often than when doing normal sewing. Use only high-quality machine needles, and start each new project with a new needle. Check your manual for the size, type, and brand of needle recommended for your machine to prevent poor quality and/or skipped stitches. This information is often found imprinted in the bobbin area of the machine.

Most people who use machines have little knowledge of needles. Below are illustrations of a needle and terms used to describe it.

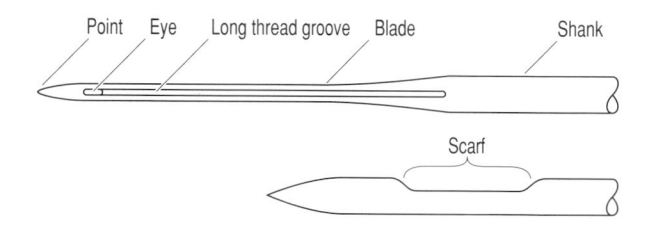

Point Eye Long thread groove Blade Shank

Scarf

Sewing machine needle terms

Hold a large sewing machine needle and examine it. Notice that the needle is flat on one side of the shank, and has a long groove on the opposite side. Run your fingernail down the long thread groove. This groove allows the thread to be protected within the needle while penetrating the material. The other side will hold the thread as it goes through the material. The thread slides through the grooved side and the eye, and because it is pinched from behind, it creates a loop behind the needle as the needle rises. This loop and the scarf (the hollowed out area on the back of the needle) allow the hook point of the shuttle to pass between the thread and the needle, locking the stitch.

Needle sizes are determined by measuring the width of the needle blade. The European system is widely accepted, but for reference, the U.S. equivalents are shown below.

Diameter in mm.	Metric/U.S.
0.65 x 100	65 / 9
0.9 x 100	90 / 14
1.1 x 100	110 / 18

Lightweight Fabrics			Mediumweight Fabrics			Heavyweight Fabrics		
60	65	70	75	80	90	100	110	120
8	9	10	11	12	14	16	18	20

Size comparisons between metric (top) and U.S.

There are many sizes and varieties of needles. Most textiles are sewn with round point needles. Needles with cutting points are only used for sewing leather and similar materials. The diagram below shows the most common types of needles available (information courtesy of the Schmetz Needle Company).

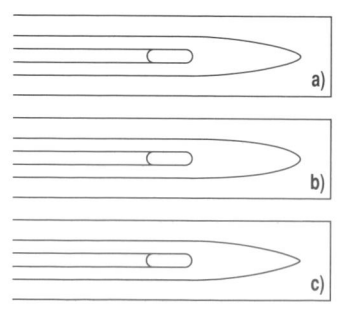

a)

b)

c)

Most commonly used needle points
a) Universal ballpoint (705 H)
b) Medium ballpoint (705H SUK)
c) Acute round point (705 HJ)

The choice of the most suitable round point needle depends on the characteristics of the fabric to be sewn, such as woven or knitted; its fiber content, such as natural, blended, or synthetic; and the desired strength and appearance of the seam. Almost all sewing machine needles are now considered semi-ballpoint or ballpoint, all being round point needles. The type of round needle point has little influence on the resistance of the fabric to the penetration of the needle. Ballpoint needles do not pierce the threads of the material but penetrate the gaps between the threads. *The coarser the fabric thread, the more the point must be rounded.*

Most fabrics can be sewn satisfactorily with a needle having a slightly rounded point (a semi-ballpoint needle). This needle is known as the *Universal* point and is manufactured with a light rounding of the point for normal sewing of woven fabrics. This needle separates the threads of the fabric and does not pierce the individual threads, which may damage the fabric. The 705H Universal needle is the most versatile as it is suitable for knits or woven fabric and is available in sizes 60–120.

Fabrics that are very easily damaged, such as synthetic knitted materials, need a more rounded point, or medium ballpoint, for best results. Schmetz identifies these needles by the letters SES and SUK. The medium ballpoint needle pushes the threads aside without perforating them, preventing snags and runs in the material.

Elastic materials with rubber or elastic threads require needles with special or heavy ballpoints. These are labeled SKL or SKF. These points also push the threads aside without perforating them. When sewing difficult projects and materials, experiment with correct needle size and point form to eliminate skipped stitches.

When sewing a tight or coarsely woven fabric with a ballpoint needle, a slight zigzag appearance may result as the needle deflects off the threads instead of piercing them. The acute round point of the 705HJ needle, also known as a "jeans" needle, has a sharper point which pierces the threads of the fabric, resulting in a uniform, straight stitch. This needle is designed to be used on woven fabrics and is available in sizes 70–110.

Most sewing machine manufacturers recommend Schmetz needles for best results. They are produced under very strict conditions to insure quality.

The semi-ballpoint (Universal) needles work best for satin stitch work. Do not use more rounded ballpoint needles, especially on woven fabrics. Experiment with different brands or types to see which needle gives you the very best satin stitch possible. If problems occur or persist, check with your dealer.

For most satin stitch work, a size 70/10 is recommended. If this size is not available in your brand, try an 11. You may find that when using thicker threads, such as metallics, a larger needle will be needed.

A little recognized fact about sewing machine needles is that they get very hot when passing through the fabric at a high rate of speed. In fabrics and threads made of natural fibers, the heat can rise to about 660° F. without causing damage. Heavier fabrics raise temperatures even higher. The sewing of natural fibers with natural fiber threads, using good needles, does not cause considerable heat difficulties.

When sewing with completely or partly synthetic fabric and thread, the speed of stitching must often be reduced by 30% because heat buildup in the needle will break the thread. This heat can damage the thread and fabrics, as well as weaken the needle's strength. When sewing synthetic fabrics and blends, use only spun polyester thread. The small hairs on the surface of the thread transport cooling air to the needle, carrying off the heat by the airstream which the spun thread produces. Also, the seam can pucker because the synthetic thread expands when being sewn and shrinks again when cooling down. The blue steel needle by Schmetz was developed to alleviate this problem. These needles are sold as Stretch, 130/705 H-S in sizes 75 and 90.

Thread and needle size are major considerations when starting to sew any project. The thread passes through the eye of the needle up to 37 times before being sewn into a stitch. If the thread is too large for the eye of the needle, it will shred and the stitches will not lock properly. If the thread is too small for the

Needle	65	70	80	90	100	110
Darning thread 60/2 or 50/2 or fine machine embroidery	■	■				
Embroidery thread No. 30		■	■			
Merc. cotton sewing 50/3			■	■		
Synthetic sewing thread (spun)			■	■		
Cotton wrapped polyester				■		
Coarse sewing thread				■	■	
Buttonhole (cordonnet)					■	■

Appropriate needle sizes for different size threads

needle eye, the stitch will appear sloppy and the tension will be affected. Below is a chart to help you select the proper size thread and needles for different sewing projects.

NOTE: The top of the Schmetz needle packages are magnified, making the needle sizes imprinted on the needle shank easier to read.

Appliqué Presser Foot

You need a special foot that will make all appliquéing techniques easier. It has no metal or plastic bar between the toes, in front of the needle, that can block your view of each stitch as it is being made. On the bottom side of the foot, there should be a long, deep groove the length of the foot, down the center of the foot. Optimally, this groove is flanged to allow for turning of corners and tight curves. The height of the satin stitch can pass freely under the foot without jamming. Without the groove, the foot catches on the mound of thread, and the fabric cannot be fed forward smoothly.

Various open-toe appliqué feet

If an appliqué foot is not available for your machine, one to fit your machine can often be purchased at a sewing machine shop. It is often referred to as a "buttonhole foot" or "open-toe foot." Also, you can often adapt your embroidery or decorative stitch foot by cutting out the center piece of metal or plastic and filing it smooth so that your vision is not hindered.

Light Box

A light box is not an absolute necessity, but it is a true asset when tracing or positioning pattern pieces onto another layer of fabric. It is quite expensive if purchased from an art supply store. However, one can be made at home with your sewing table or by simply placing a sheet of glass over the leaf opening of your dining room table and using a bare light bulb in a lamp on the floor underneath the glass.

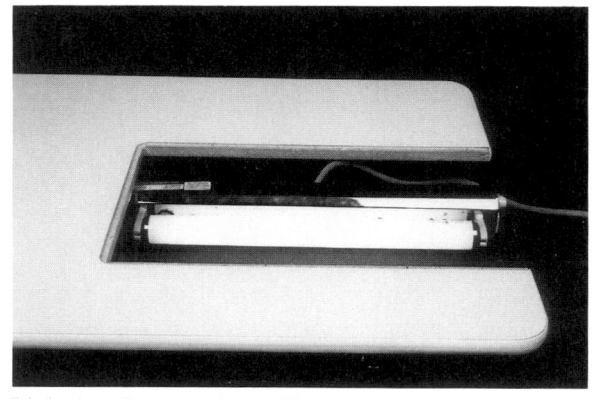

Light box from sewing table

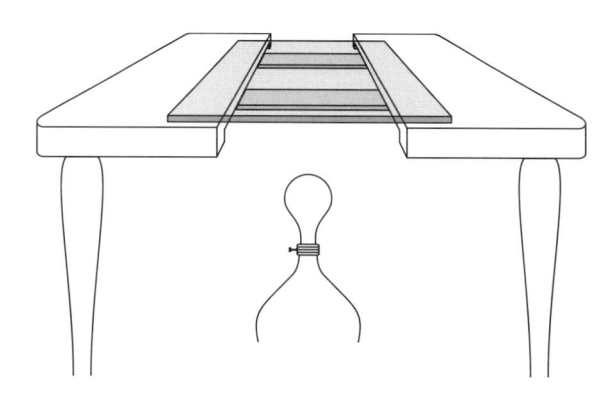

Using dining room table for light box

You could also build a wooden box and add kitchen under-counter fluorescent light sticks and a sheet of Plexiglas® to create a portable light box. You can adapt a child's Lite-Brite® toy if you have one, or a window is the old-fashioned standby.

Iron

A full-size iron is the most efficient when working on larger pieces, and a small travel iron with a sharp point is ideal for small work. If you have an old dry iron, use it as your "appliqué" iron. Its smooth surface provides more even heat distribution than a steam iron which has holes in the sole plate. Make sure that the thermostat still allows the iron to heat up sufficiently to bond fusibles.

The bottom of your iron needs to be kept clean and smooth, free of any residues of sizings and finishes from fabrics, as well as residues of the fusibles. There are commercial iron cleaners (such as Iron Off™, available at your local fabric store) that will dissolve and eliminate these residues. The ProGlide™ iron by Bernina® has a sole plate that will not scratch and that fusibles cannot stick to, making it problem free to work with fusible agents.

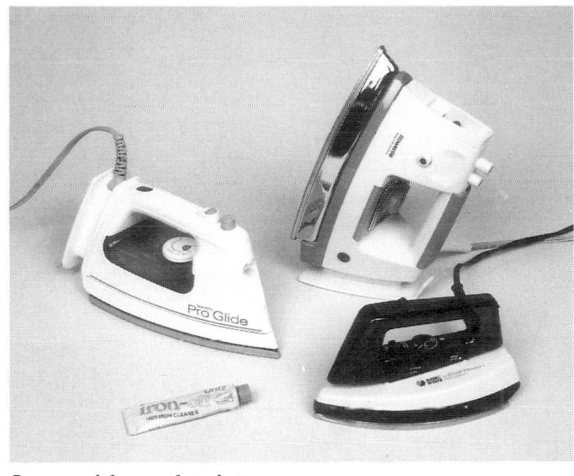

Irons with good points

A large piece of muslin or a non-stick pressing sheet covering your ironing board will protect it from residues of fusibles and transfer pencil marks so that they cannot damage garments ironed later.

CHAPTER TWO

Supplies

Threads

Satin Stitch appliqué uses a tremendous amount of thread. Be very particular about the size, brand, and quality of thread you use in your machine for these techniques. High quality thread is essential to fine stitch quality. You will be using 100% cotton thread for your beginning satin stitch techniques. Cotton threads are softer than man-made fibers and tend to untwist and spread a little on the surface, giving much better coverage without crowding the stitches. Cotton is also a more flexible fiber than polyester. This flexibility produces a smoother, more consistent satin stitch. Cotton thread also has a much lower amount of thread drag than synthetic threads, allowing your machine tensions to create a nicer looking stitch.

Purchase only machine embroidery threads for satin stitching and any other decorative work done on the machine where there is a buildup of stitches. Machine embroidery threads are 2-ply threads. They are loosely twisted, very weak and soft, and allow the stitches to build up and fill in tightly in the stitching process. Sewing threads are too bulky, too tightly twisted, and stitch unevenly and/or jam under satin stitch conditions.

NOTE: The size and ply of the thread is generally printed on the spool. An example is 60/2. The 60 stands for the size of the thread; the 2 tells how many plys are twisted together.

Several brands and sizes of machine embroidery threads are available. DMC® makes size 30 and size 50 threads, both 2-ply. Swiss/Metrosene makes Mettler embroidery thread in size 30 (yellow printing on the spool) and size 60 (green printing on spool). The larger the number, the thinner the thread. I highly recommend using the 50 weight DMC or the 60 weight Mettler for satin stitching. These quality threads are made of long-fiber cotton, which reduces snagging and breaking. They also have a consistency of diameter resulting in uniformity of stitches and less thread drag. Refer to the chart on page 14 for proper needle sizes.

Remember that the color of the thread and the width of the stitch can affect the overall appearance of the piece. When choosing your thread color, consider that a slightly darker thread will frame a piece best and cover more completely, but a lighter color will make the design seem to shine on the edges.

We will be using only size 60/2 in the bobbin, because a very thin thread in the bobbin reduces excessive buildup in the stitch. White is the most used color, but if there are tension problems, matching the bobbin thread to the top color may be necessary. And if both sides of the project will be seen, definitely match top and bottom threads. There is now a size 80/2 thread available that would also be an excellent choice for

Various embroidery threads used in appliqué

bobbin thread. This thread is being used for French Hand Sewing by machine.

TIP: Basting cotton is often sold for bobbin thread for machine art work, but I would not recommend it. It is a very short-fiber thread (which creates a lot of lint in the machine), its diameter is uneven, and the thickness of the thread causes excessive buildup. Mettler's fine embroidery, 60 weight/2-ply is far superior.

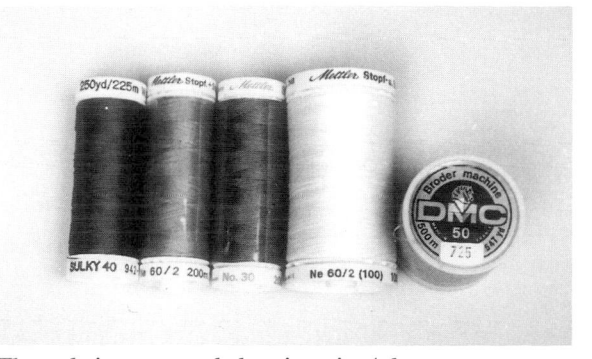

Thread size on spool showing size/ply

Scissors

A large amount of cutting is necessary in appliqué, and high quality scissors will make it much easier. I suggest that you invest in Gingher® scissors for this type of work. There are several varieties available, depending on your preferences. Small 5" scissors and the 5" tailor-point scissors make easy work of cutting small, detailed shapes, and their small, pointed blades are easy to control. Shears in 7" and 8" lengths cut larger shapes much faster and more smoothly.

Gingher appliqué scissors are used when trimming around a stitched item where cutting very close to the stitching is necessary. They are mainly used for reverse appliqué techniques and are not meant to be

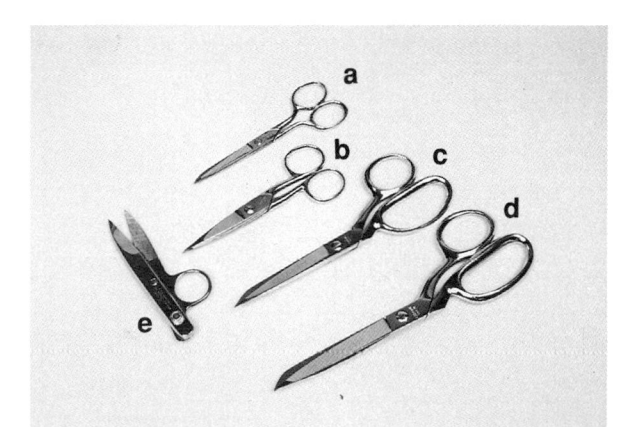

a) 5" scissors b) 5" tailor point scissors c) 7" shears d) 8" shears e) Thread clips

general purpose scissors. The duckbill-shaped blade lies flat on the fabric to create resistance for the cutting blade when cutting close to the stitching. Thread clips are handy for clipping thread tails. One final note: Sharp scissors are a must!

TIP: When cutting, practice moving the paper or fabric, not the scissors. This will leave smoother edges. Also, try taking large bites with the blades to give a longer, more continuous cut. Small chops leave uneven edges.

Fabrics

Appliqués consist of fabric pieces applied onto a fabric background. Beginners of satin stitch techniques will find sturdy woven 100% cotton fabrics the easiest background to use. In general, the appliqué pieces should be lighter in weight than the background of your project.

If the item you are appliquéing is going to be laundered, decide whether to preshrink it. If you are appliquéing onto a preshrunk garment, you will need to preshrink the appliqué fabrics. If the item is going to be quilted, you may choose not to preshrink to obtain an antique look from the work. Often the fabrics of appliqué will shrink in varying degrees, causing unsightly puckers and wrinkles. If necessary, make a sample with the chosen fabrics and wash to see how they will react.

If the fabrics appear limp and hard to work with, a little spray sizing will add body. Fabrics of 100% cotton are easiest to work with when applying heat-fusing products. Be careful of heat-sensitive fabrics when using fusibles. They may not be able to withstand the hot temperature required for the fusing process.

Grainline is not particularly important on smaller appliqués, but when large pieces are worked with, match the grainline of the appliqué to the grainline of the background fabric. This is especially important if (a) you are going to wear or hang the finished product, or (b) it is not going to be quilted within the appliqué itself.

Iron-On Interfacing

Lightweight, fusible interfacing in nonwoven form is one product that can be used for appliqué. This interfacing needs to be soft and flexible. It will fuse to the back of the appliqué fabric, adding strength and stability and keeping all edges from fraying. Once the

appliqué is stitched, it is not flat and stiff as with fusible webbings. This interfacing shrinks more than fabrics, causing unsightly puckers within the appliqué, so be sure to preshrink it before working with it. To preshrink, submerge it into a basin of warm water. (Do not wring or twist.) Hang it over a rod or hanger, fusing sides out, and allow to drip-dry.

You can experiment with nonwovens, wovens, and knitted interfacings to see which you prefer. Different weights can be used for different weight fabrics and effects. Practice your stitch techniques using many different products to decide which product will give you your desired end results.

NOTE: *There is a professional-grade appliqué interfacing available from many stores that teach sewing machine arts, or from some sewing machine dealers. It is used in the garment industry for appliquéd garments.*

Fusible Webs
(Stitch Witchery™, Fine Fuse™)

Fusing agents come in various forms, each requiring a different method for applying them to fabrics. Purchase as many of these products as you can locate and experiment with them to discover which ones provide the results you are looking for. There really isn't one that is better than the others, but they vary in stiffness and in ease of handling.

Stitch Witchery and Fine Fuse both come by the yard and are durable fusible webs. Stitch Witchery gives a firm, almost stiff, feel to the finished item, whereas Fine Fuse leaves the item soft and pliable. Both Stitch Witchery and Fine Fuse launder very well. There is sufficient adhesive agent to hold the fabrics together if directions are followed carefully. Tumble dry the items only on low-heat settings.

When Stitch Witchery was first introduced, it was messy and difficult to work with. You had to cut the fusible the exact size as the appliqué, carefully place them together on the background fabric, then press. The fabrics usually slipped, leaving a gooey mess on the iron as well as the fabrics.

TIP: *If you do get fusing agents on the sole plate of your iron, remove them with Iron Off iron cleaner.*

When Fine Fuse was introduced, along with it came non-stick pressing sheets. These sheets of heat-resistant material create iron-on fabric and make it possible to work with these fusibles without getting the fusible on the iron and ironing board. The pressing sheets are reusable, long-lasting, transparent, and temperature-safe. They come in several sizes and two different grades. The professional grade is more durable and long-lasting, and the larger the sheet, the more useful it is.

Fusible webs melt between two layers of fabric, creating a permanent bond. Care must be taken when working with these products, as they tend to stray and easily melt onto irons and ironing board covers. They used to be tedious to work with because they had to be cut to the exact size as the appliqué itself. The Teflon pressing sheet described below has made them much more acceptable and easy to handle, with very good results. A flatter, stiffer appliqué is produced from fusible webs, compared to the free and soft appliqué produced from interfacing.

Paper-Backed Fusible Webs
(Wonder-Under™,
HeatnBond® Lite, AppliHesive)

These products came after the fusible webs. The application of a paper backing makes pattern tracing and cutting much easier. Also, a separate pressing sheet is usually not needed.

Wonder-Under is a paper-backed fusible web that can be used instead of Stitch Witchery or Fine Fuse. It is quick and easy to handle but tends to have less adhesive agent. This can present problems if laundering is frequent. Again, make test samples of the various products, and wash several times before choosing the product you will use on a given project.

HeatnBond is a fairly new product. It is a 100% solid sheet of glue for a very strong bond. This product is ideal for bonding delicate fabrics and lightweight materials where a lower temperature is necessary with a shorter pressing time. It is more washable and dry cleanable than the webs.

These products came after the fusible webs, making them easier to use. A paper backing has been applied to make pattern tracing and cutting much easier. Also, a separate pressing sheet is usually not needed.

AppliHesive is a heavy duty, paper-backed fusible product that feels like plastic. It is the same product used on commercial jean patches and embroidered iron-on decals. You can make your own patches with it, or use it to give items a stiff, durable finish.

Non-Stick Pressing Sheets
(Easy Way Appliqué®)

These sheets made of heat-resistant material can be ironed onto directly, so that applying fusible webs to fabrics is much simpler than before. We no longer have to cut the pieces separately, then realign them and hope they don't move as the iron comes down. Now the design is drawn directly onto the fusing agent, then placed onto a piece of fabric, and covered by the pressing sheet. The iron is on the pressing sheet, fusing the web onto a piece of fabric. The fusing agent cannot stick to the sheet, so it can be easily peeled upon cooling. Then the appliqué is cut out on the line.

Pressing sheets are translucent and are used in various steps for preparing fabric. You can buy them in a variety of sizes, as well as by the yard (a large size is handy for larger projects). A professional grade pressing sheet will last for years. Any residue left on the pressing sheet from the fusing webs should be brushed off to prevent it from getting on the iron or a fabric where it does not belong. Keep your pressing sheet clean.

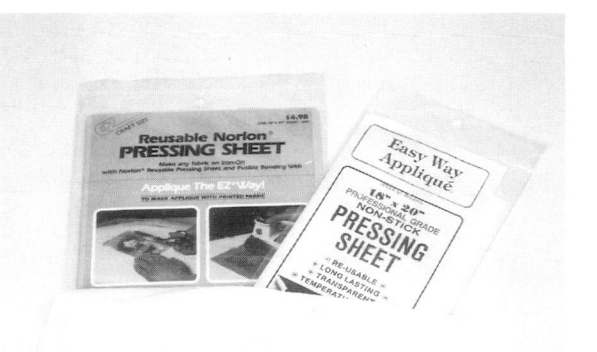

Various pressing sheets

Fabric-Basting Glue Sticks
(suggested brand names: Aleene's™, Dennison, Collins, Dritz)

This textile glue comes in a stick form similar to a lipstick and can be found in fabric and quilt stores. It is made from a nontoxic and water-soluble glue with a touch of Teflon. It is useful for holding anything that you might otherwise have to pin—especially points, corners, and curved edges. Tiny pieces that cannot be pinned are easier to handle with glue sticks. Be careful not to use paper glue sticks because they drag on the fabric, making it difficult to spread the glue evenly, and they often discolor the fabric.

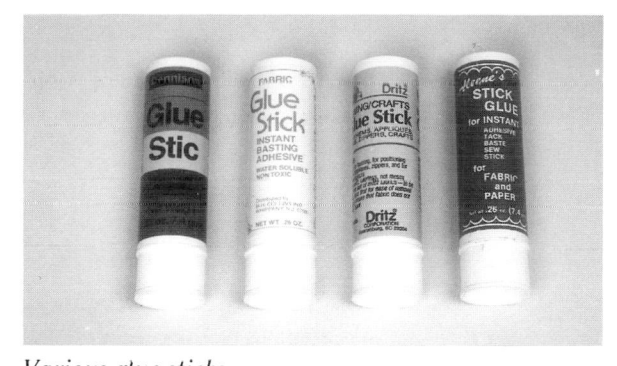

Various glue sticks

Hot Iron Transfer Pencil
(Sulky® Iron-On Transfer Pen, Noblot Ink Pencil®)

These convenient marking devices and a hot dry iron give us a quick method for transferring designs from pattern to fabric. The Sulky Iron-On Transfer Pens are felt-tip markers in various colors that transfer permanently and easily onto any surface where a hot iron can be used. They leave a bright, bold line in a variety of colors to meet different fabric needs. They do not bleed and can be transferred 3–5 times with one application. Patterns can be traced onto almost any paper for transferring.

A transfer pencil called Noblot Ink Pencil (also called Bottle of Ink in a Pencil) is a highly recommended non-wax pencil that draws on like a regular pencil, but leaves a blue line when heated. (Wax-based transfer pencils are available in a variety of colors and are found in fabric and hobby stores. But be careful when using these, because the wax tends to smear onto other fabrics, or it can show through the layers.) Trace the pattern designs onto ordinary tissue paper with this pencil for the most durable transfer. The actual technique will be covered in the lessons.

Various hot iron transfer pencils and pens

Stabilizers

There are several nonwoven nylon or polyester products sold as background stabilizers. These products are not fusible and do not become a permanent part of the appliqué. Instead, they are used underneath the background fabric to give extra body and support for the satin stitches to prevent tunneling and puckering. Products such as Do-Sew® have to be trimmed away with scissors after stitching. More preferable are the tearable products, such as Tear-Away and Stitch and Tear™. They leave a nicer finish and save a lot of time. Stitch and Tear should be used only on durable, heavier-weight fabrics. Tear-Away comes in "soft" and "crisp" and is gentler on the finer and lighter-weight fabrics when being removed. Tear-Away is soft and pliable and easy to manipulate in larger sizes while working on large projects.

Freezer paper is another good stabilizer. The plastic side can be ironed onto the back of the background fabric and then torn off after stitching. Once ironed on, it helps eliminate shifting and fabric stretching. It is stiff and best suited to satin stitching smaller projects.

The latest products to hit the appliqué market are Press and Tear and Sulky's Totally Stable. These are iron-on tear-away products with a plastic coating on one side, like freezer paper. They keep knits and unstable fabrics from stretching while stitching. They also eliminate shifting, sliding, and puckering of fabrics while being stitched and leave no residue when excess is torn away. Now you can iron a soft, flexible stabilizer onto larger projects as well as onto sweatshirt fleece and knits. It sticks like freezer paper until you tear it away, and it keeps its flexibility while working.

Aqua-Solv© and Solvy™

These products have been used in machine arts for several years and are now finding their way into quilting. They are water-soluble embroidery facings made of a gelatinous substance. They are easy to use and dissolve by spraying or soaking in cool water. Use them for placement marking of detail lines for Satin Stitch appliqué.

Water-soluable embroidery facings

CHAPTER THREE

Fabric Preparation— Let's Get Started

Appliqué fabrics can be prepared many different ways, with varying end results. Of the variety of products available, each gives the project a different appearance and texture. Experiment with different fusing webs, interfacings, and adhesives to determine your preferences.

Working with Patterns

When working with the interfacing technique, you make a paper pattern using tissue paper. When working with fusible webs, the pattern can be drawn directly onto the web or the paper backing of the web. Each method requires you to understand the principles of mirror image or reverse image. Be sure to mark your patterns "front" and "back" so that you will not be confused when working with different techniques. If the pattern is not traced properly, the picture or design will be facing the opposite direction of the original

pattern. Specific instructions are given with each process. Trace the pattern onto a sheet of translucent paper with a fine felt-tip marker. This will protect your original from markings when tracing onto fusible webs and will make the pattern easier to trace from the back side for reverse image tracings.

Look carefully at the pattern. Many pieces can remain large shapes, and the detail lines stitched in, instead of cutting separate pieces of fabric for every detail. An example is the flower below. The piece of fabric is cut using the outside lines, and the petal segments are stitched in.

Wherever two pattern pieces come together, one of the pieces must be under the other. The underlapping edge needs to have an extension of ⅛"–³⁄₁₆". We never want to "butt" two raw edges together. The underlapping piece is the one that appears to be behind as you look at the pattern. Often, you will need to consider that lighter fabrics should underlap darker ones.

Identify outside cutting lines

Pattern with extensions drawn in

Draw these extensions onto the pattern in red before tracing the pattern. This will remind you to add them to each pattern piece where they are needed while tracing.

How To Use Iron-On Interfacing

When making only one item from a pattern, trace the designs directly onto the smooth side of the interfacing before fusing the interfacing onto the back of the appliqué fabric. You will need to trace the pattern from the BACK side of the pattern—reverse image—onto the non-fusible side of the interfacing. Trace the lines slightly outside the pattern lines so that you can cut the line away when cutting out the shape. Don't forget to add any extensions needed for underlapping pieces.

Tracing designs onto interfacing directly

If you need to make several of the same design, make hot iron transfers of the pattern pieces. Tissue paper works well with hot-iron transfer pencils. It will not scorch and turn brittle when heat is applied in the transferring process. If using Iron On Transfer Pens, almost any type of writing paper will work.

Tracing cutting lines with transfer pencil

Trace from the FRONT side of the pattern for this technique, and press down when tracing to get a solid, narrow line from the pencil. The pens will give a fluid line like a felt tip marker. Trace only the cutting lines with the hot iron transfer pencil. Next, with a regular pencil, trace the inside design lines that will be stitched only, not cut. We will work with these later.

Tracing inside design lines with regular pencil

Fuse the interfacing onto the wrong side of the different appliqué fabrics, following manufacturer's directions.

Fusing interfacing to fabrics

Lay the tissue paper pattern, transfer-pencil-side-down, on the interfaced side of the fabric. Hold in place and apply a hot (cotton setting) iron onto the tissue paper. Make sure that the iron temperature is not too hot for the fabrics that you have chosen: The transfer pencil works best with a hot iron, but adjustments need to be made for more delicate fabrics. As you are heating the pattern with the iron, peel up a corner to check on your progress. You need a line only dark enough to see to cut. Do not overheat and make a dark line. By keeping the line light, you should be able to repeat this process four to eight times before the transfer wears out.

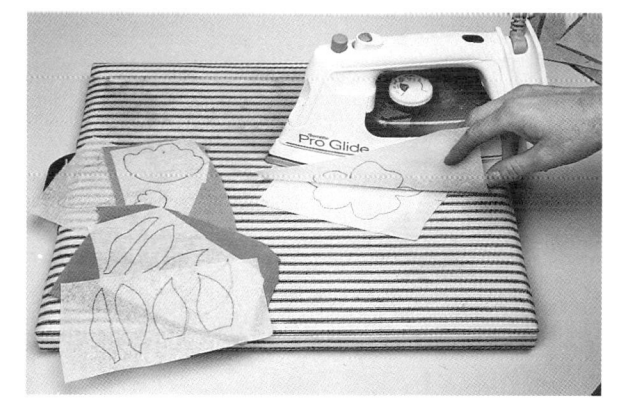

Transferring designs onto interfacing

Cut the pieces out, just inside the lines, using very smooth, even strokes with the scissors. If there are jags and uneven edges, the stitching will also be uneven, as you can only see what is at the needle when sewing. The smoother the cutting, the neater the stitching.

Cut out pieces smoothly

Once the pieces are cut, go back to your pattern pieces and retrace with the hot iron transfer pencil—on the opposite side of the tissue paper—the inside design lines that you traced with a regular pencil. This is now an embroidery transfer. Align the pattern on the right side of the cut fabric piece, matching the cutting

Retrace design lines with transfer pencil

lines with the original transfer lines, and press. The new transfer lines will stamp onto the right side of fabric, giving placement lines for detail stitching. *Keep these lines as light as possible.*

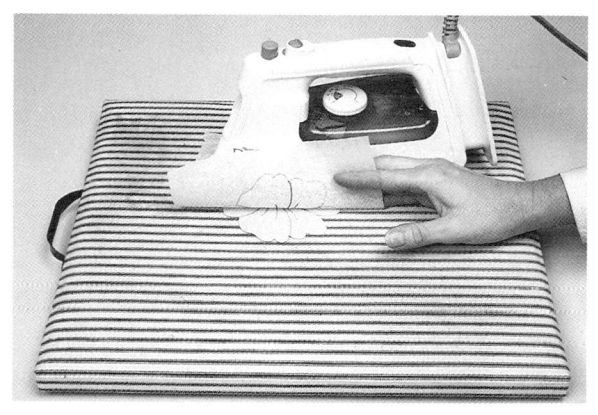

Transfer design lines onto front of appliqué

If you don't care to use the transfer pencil this way, trace the lines onto the fabric with chalk or a washout felt-tip pen, using a light box or a window. You could also use Aqua Solv, following the directions on the package.

Using light box to trace lines

How To Use Fusible Webs

Prepare the pattern for appliqué interfacing as discussed on page 23. This is also a raw edge application, and extensions need to be added to the pattern in advance. Draw the desired shapes onto the fusible, using a felt-tip pen or marking pencil. Draw carefully so that you do not tear the web. Cut apart the different units, but do not cut the designs on their lines.

Draw designs directly onto web

Cut units apart

Place the pressing sheet on the ironing board. Lay the appliqué fabric right-side-down on one half of the pressing sheet.

Pressing sheet on ironing surface

Next lay the fusing web, reverse image facing you, on top of the fabric.

Fabric wrong side up—fusing web reverse image

Cover both the fabric and fusing web with the remaining half of the pressing sheet.

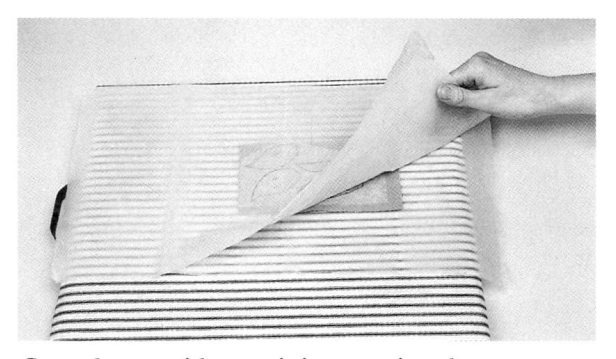

Cover layers with remaining pressing sheet

With your iron set on the wool setting, press the layers for 5–10 seconds. (Do not slide the iron.) The adhesive cannot adhere to the pressing sheet, so it can only adhere to the fabric. Allow the pressing sheet to cool, then peel it away from the fused fabric. You now have fusible fabric.

Press sandwich

Peel pressing sheet away from fusible

Cut out the design on the line, handling the item very carefully to avoid stretching the edges, which causes fraying. You now have an "iron-on" appliqué.

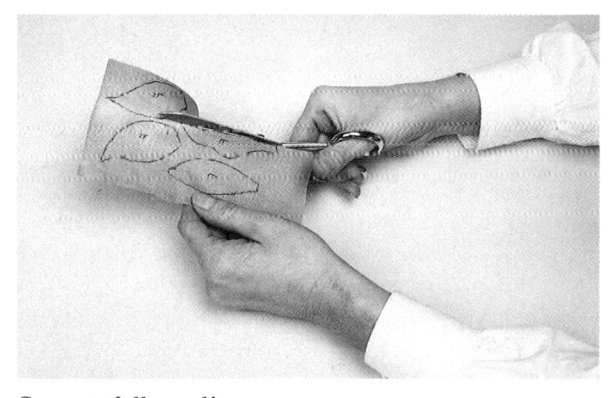

Cut carefully on line

Position the appliqué onto the item it is to be stitched to. With your iron on the steam and wool setting, press for 10 seconds. If you are using a dry iron, use a wet press cloth. The non-stick pressing sheet is not necessary for this step, but the use of a damp press cloth will strengthen the bonding process.

Stitch all raw edges.

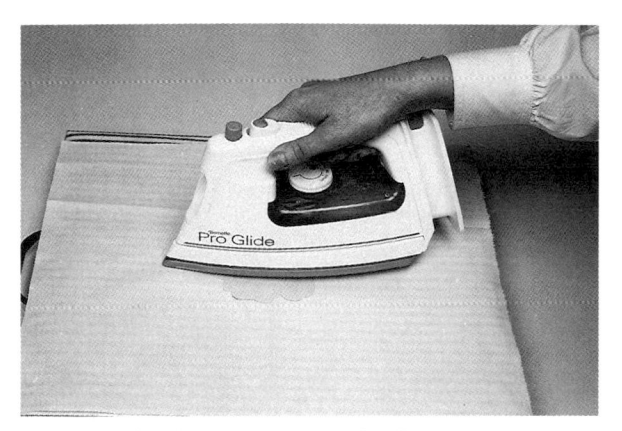

Fuse appliqué to background fabric

How To Use Paper Backed Fusible Webs

Wonder-Under or HeatnBond

TIP: Carefully read instruction sheet that comes with each product before starting. Follow suggested pressing temperatures and times for each product.

Start by tracing the design shape directly onto the paper side of Wonder-Under. *Remember to draw the design in reverse image.*

Trace design onto paper side

To protect the ironing board from any stray edge of fusible, position the non-stick pressing sheet onto the ironing board. Lay your appliqué fabric right-side-down on the pressing sheet.

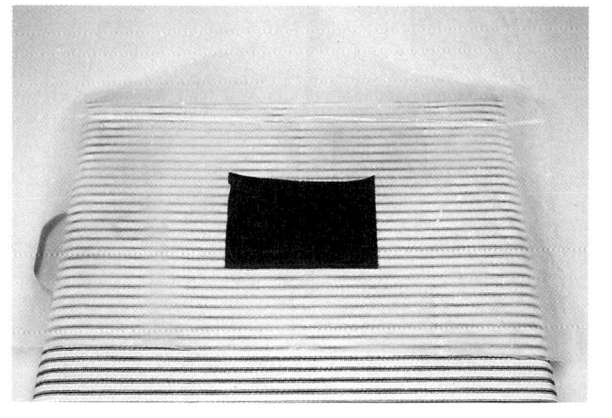

Fabric face-down on pressing sheet

Place the rough side of Wonder-Under against the wrong side of the appliqué fabric. Press for three seconds with a hot dry iron. (Do not slide iron.) Let the fabric cool.

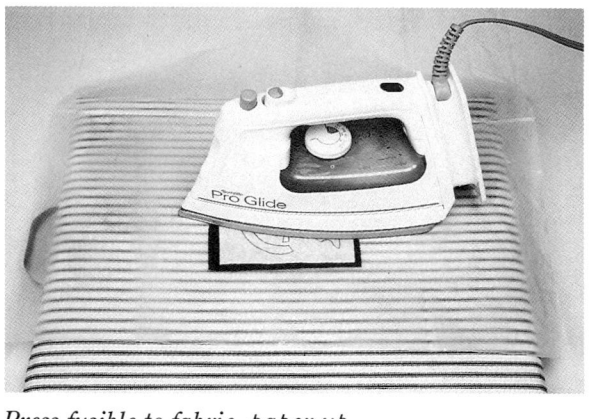

Press fusible to fabric, paper up

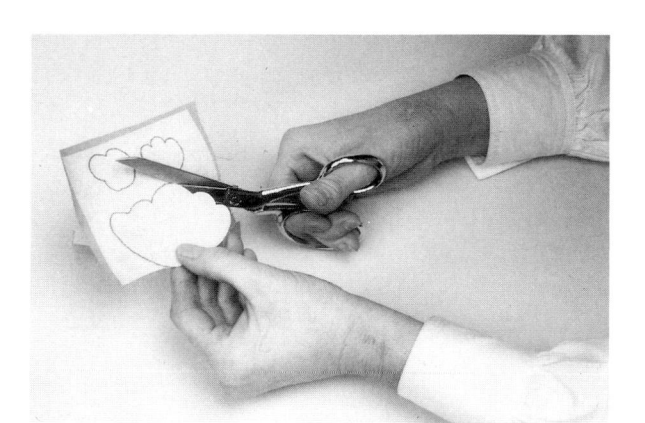

Cut carefully

Cut out the item on the line, making very smooth, even cuts. Handle the pieces carefully.

Gently peel off the paper backing, taking care not to stretch the edges of the appliqué. Place the appliqué, adhesive-side-down, onto the right side of the background fabric and press with a hot iron. The appliqué is now ready to stitch.

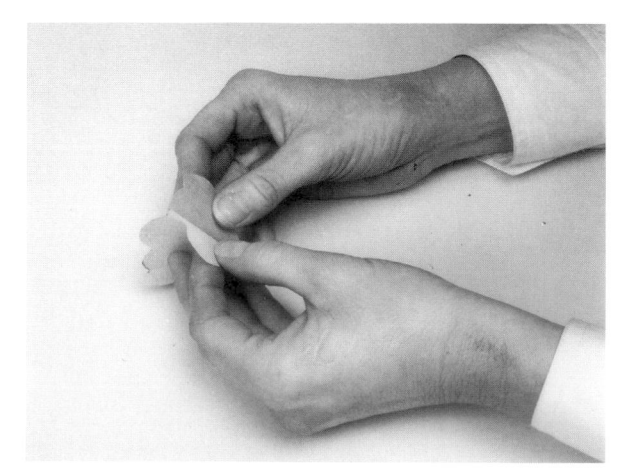

Peel paper

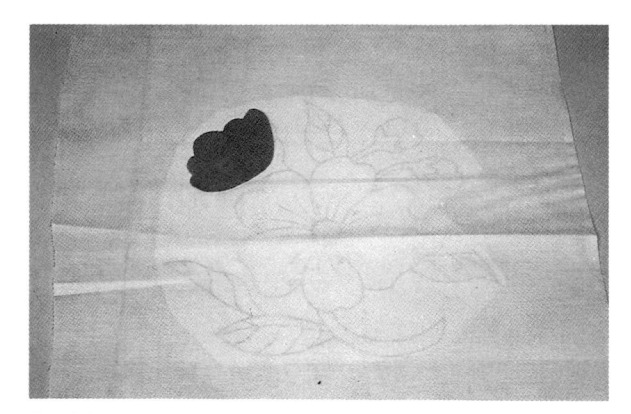

Position onto background fabric

AppliHesive Appliqué Film

Use a dry iron, set between wool and cotton (350°). Lay a brown paper bag on the ironing board to protect the ironing board and to act as a heat conductor. Lay the appliqué fabric right-side-down on the bag.

Brown paper on ironing surface

Draw the design elements onto the paper side of the AppliHesive, tracing them in reverse image. Do not cut out the design before applying AppliHesive. Lay the AppliHesive shiny-side-down on the fabric. Press 15 seconds. (Do not slide the iron.) If a large appliqué is being done, lift the iron and reposition.

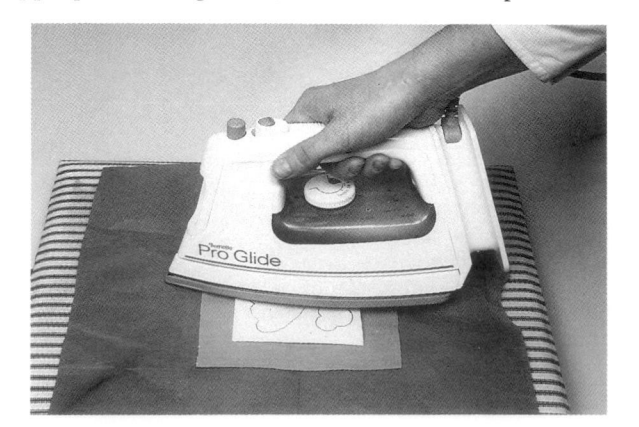

Press fusible onto fabric

Cut out the design and remove the paper backing. The shiny film should be visible on the back of the appliqué. Position the appliqué on the backing fabric.

Press to begin the fusing process, then turn the piece over to the wrong side. Press on the back of the background fabric for approximately 15–20 seconds. Again, do not slide the iron. It may take a little longer for the appliqué to adhere tightly because of the extra layer of fabric.

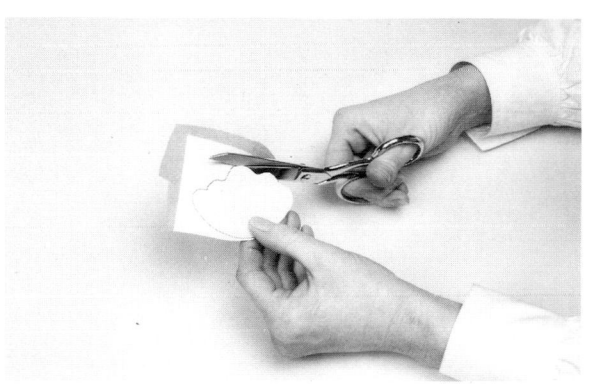

Cut design lines carefully

Peel off paper backing

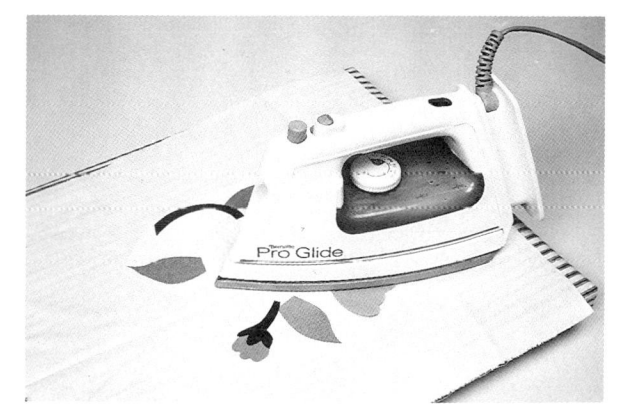

Place on background—press

CHAPTER FOUR

Machine Preparation Before You Stitch

Before starting any sewing project, be sure to clean and oil your machine. A well maintained machine will give you many hours of pleasure. Thoroughly clean the bobbin area and the feed dog area with a lint brush. Often the smallest amount of lint or debris will cause the machine to skip stitches and have tension problems. Use brushes and pipe cleaners to remove lint from every reachable area. Tweezers can be used to remove caught threads, but otherwise avoid using metal tools to clean with, as they can create burrs that will cause thread breakage. Remove the needle plate and clean the lint from between the feed dogs. Scrub the feed dogs with a toothbrush. Use a vacuum to suck away loose particles, then use the blower or canned air to blow out the tiny particles not removed by suction.

Check the tension disks on the machine as well as the pressure spring on the bobbin (the clip that thread goes under when threading the bobbin) for any lint or residue. Clean between the disks with a pipe cleaner. The pressure spring on the bobbin case may contain lint or pieces of thread that can cause tensions to vary and cause poor stitches. Clean the inside of the bobbin case, as lint buildup can cause the bobbin to spin unevenly, also affecting the quality of the stitches.

Lightly oil the shuttle and race of the bobbin area every time you clean it. Use only high quality pure oil, purchased from your sewing machine dealer, that has no detergents. Regular machine oils will eventually cause the mechanisms to lock up. Do not spray silicon or products such as WD40 into the machine because they overspray, and many parts need to be completely free of lubricant.

Once a month, if you are sewing a great deal or doing a lot of appliqué work, put a drop of oil on the needle bar (take the needle out before oiling). Let the machine run for two minutes after applying the oil, then let it sit for 10 minutes so the excess oil can drain off. When not sewing, lower the needle into soft cotton fabric so that any excess oil can wick into the fabric.

Clean the body of the machine, and wax it with a high quality car wax for enameled steel parts and a hot tub wax for the plastic parts. Keep the machine covered when not in use to prevent accumulation of dust and dirt particles.

After you have oiled the machine, put in the proper needle. Check in your manual to see if the flat side of the needle goes to the back or to the side. When inserting the needle, push it up until it hits the stop, then tighten the screw. Do not apply too much pressure on the needle clamp screw, because you could easily break off the point that holds the needle in place. Tighten until firm. If the needle is not inserted properly, the machine will skip stitches, if it will sew at all. When sewing, listen to the sound of your machine. Any time that you hear a punching sound, stop and change the needle. A dull or bent needle can damage the machine.

Put the open-toe appliqué foot on your machine so you can test tension, stitch width, and stitch length without jammed stitches.

Wind several bobbins with size 60/2 thread before sewing. When winding the bobbin, be sure that it is winding smoothly and evenly, and that the thread is being wound tight. Loose, unevenly wound bobbins cause poor stitch quality.

Identify the tension adjustment dial on your machine. When doing any type of machine art work, you need to become comfortable with tension adjustments to make the machine work properly with different types and combinations of threads.

There is no magic about thread tension, and many service calls can be eliminated if you have a thorough understanding of how tension works.

Sew a row of stitches in two layers of fabric. Correct tension is evident when both threads are linked together in the center of the layered fabrics (figure a). Figure b shows the bottom thread being pulled tight. This could indicate that the top thread is too loose or the bobbin thread is too tight. Figure c shows the top thread being pulled tight. This could indicate that the top thread is too tight, or the bobbin thread is too loose.

Effects of bobbin tension adjustments

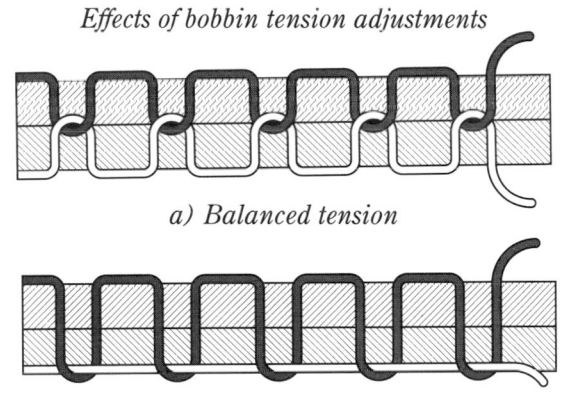

a) Balanced tension

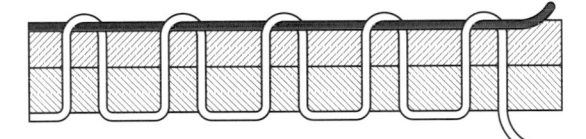

b) Top tension too loose or bobbin too tight

c) Top tension too tight or bobbin too loose

When excess thread is looped in the bobbin area, it may not indicate a bobbin thread problem. The top thread might be too loose, allowing the race mechanism to gather the loose thread loop on the underneath side of the fabric and preventing stitches from forming properly.

For the appliqué techniques in this book, you will be using a fairly tight bobbin tension and a slightly loosened top tension. This allows the bobbin thread to deliberately pull the top thread to the underside, giving the stitches on top a satiny, even appearance.

You can check your own bobbin tension and correct it if necessary. With the high speed and long

duration of sewing times required for appliqué, bobbin tension can fluctuate. Knowing how to check and adjust it can save a lot of time and irritation.

Thread a full bobbin into the bobbin case. Make sure it is threaded properly (check your manual to see if the bobbin spins clockwise or counter-clockwise). Test for normal tension by letting the bobbin case hang down freely by the thread. It must not slide down by its own weight, but when you jerk your hand lightly upward, yo-yo style, it should gently fall. If it doesn't move at all, the tension is tight. If it falls easily, it is loose.

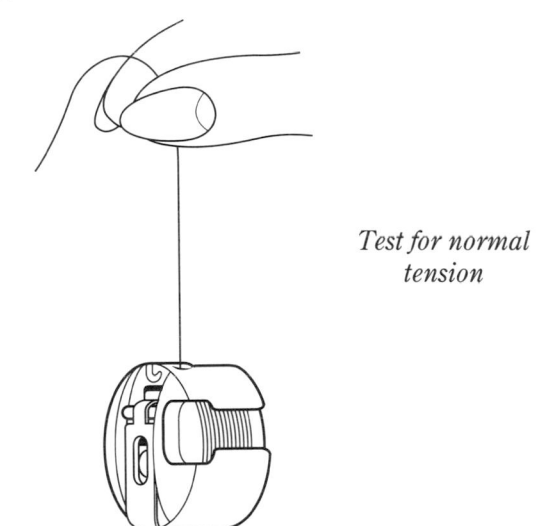

Test for normal tension

Adjust the tension by adjusting the large screw on the tension clip. Turn it to the right to tighten, and to the left to loosen. Adjust in very small increments until the tension is correct. Read the screw like a clock, and move only one hour at a time. Test this with different sizes and types of thread; you will find that the proper setting of the tension will be different for different threads.

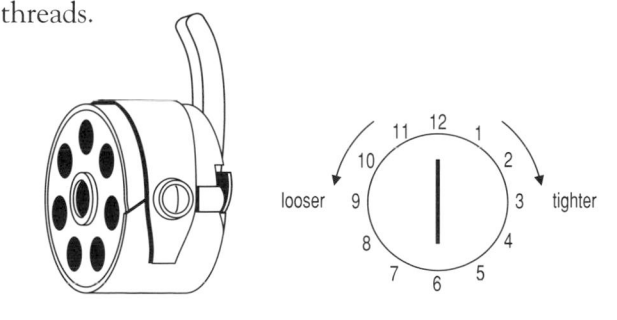

Tension screw—right to tighten, left to loosen

Incorrect tension is why your machine does not always sew properly. Polyester threads have more thread drag than cottons, requiring the tensions to be looser. The tension also needs to be loosened when heavier

threads are used. When we do machine art work such as appliqué, using very thin size 60 or 80 2-ply threads, the tension will need to be tightened to get the proper drag on the thread. When trying to achieve a perfect satin stitch, the top thread should be pulled down to the underside. This requires a tighter than normal bobbin and a looser setting on top.

TIP: If you are using a Bernina, insert the thread into the hole in the finger of the bobbin case. This will automatically tighten the tension.

If you find that you need to change your bobbin tension, consider purchasing another bobbin case and marking it with fingernail polish. Then this bobbin case can be changed whenever you need anything other than normal tension, and the other case is set for your favorite thread and normal sewing.

While testing the tension with different threads, get familiar with the position of the stitch width knob or button. While sewing, move the width knob from narrow to wider and back to narrow to get the feel of adjusting the stitch width while sewing. You will be doing quite a bit of this as you taper points. Be careful not to move the length knob by mistake.

Next, adjust the stitch length knob or button while sewing. Leave your hands off the fabric, allowing the feed dogs to do all the feeding. Shorten the stitch to where it will not move at all, up to a long stitch. Now fine-tune the stitch length so that it will fill in a heavy satin stitch with no gaps between the stitches, but also without jamming and stopping.

Repeat these tests several times, each time using different threads and needles and different combinations of threads. The machine settings for both width and length will be different for every different thread that you sew with. Once you are familiar with the basic functions of tension, width and length of stitches, and thread and needle sizes, you will be able to manipulate your machine to give you the look you are trying to achieve.

NOTE: When testing machine stitches, always have a stabilizer under the background fabric.

COMMON FAULTS AND SUGGESTED CORRECTIONS
Listed are problems most often responsible for poor sewing performance

Unattractive Stitches
1. The needle is incorrectly inserted.
2. The needle is bent or blunt. Change the needle.
3. The thread tension is not correct.
4. Needle point is not correct. Refer to needle and thread chart.
5. The machine is incorrectly threaded. Check the manual.
6. The needle, thread and fabric do not correspond.
7. The lower thread is not the same thickness as the upper thread.
8. The bobbin thread is incorrectly inserted in the bobbin case.
9. Lint or thread is wrapped around the spindle of the shuttle. Clean it out.
10. Poor quality thread.

Needle Breakage
1. The needle is incorrectly inserted.
2. Overassisting the machine in feeding the fabric through. Do not pull.
3. The needle is not the right size.
4. Bobbin is overfilled.
5. Tension is too tight on upper thread.
6. Thread is entangled on spool pin.

Upper Thread Breaks or Shreds
1. The needle is incorrectly inserted.
2. The needle is bent or blunt. Change the needle.
3. The upper thread is incorrectly threaded.
4. The upper thread is too tightly tensioned.
5. The thread is knotted.
6. The needle and thread do not correspond.
7. The hole in the throat plate is chipped or has sharp edges. Polish or change.
8. The needle groove or needle eye has sharp edges. Change the needle.
9. Thread is entangled on the spool pin.

Lower Thread Breaks
1. The bobbin case is incorrectly inserted.
2. The lower thread is incorrectly threaded.
3. The lower thread is too tightly tensioned.
4. The bobbin is wound too full.
5. The throat plate hole is damaged.
6. Lint or thread is wrapped around the spindle of the shuttle. Clean it out.

Stitch Length Varies
1. The feed dog is choked by dust and dirt. Clean with a small brush.
2. The presser foot pressure is not properly adjusted.

CHAPTER FIVE

Learning the Stitch Techniques

How To Set Your Machine

Now that you have become comfortable with the functions of the machine and how to change them for different effects, you need to set your machine to do a perfect satin stitch. The needle position for the majority of Satin Stitch appliqué is in the center position. Put the open-toe appliqué foot on the machine, thread the bobbin and top with the appropriate embroidery threads (refer to Chapter Two), and place a size 70 needle in the machine.

A satin stitch consists of narrow zigzag stitches set close enough to appear as a solid line, but not so close that they bunch up and jam in front of the foot. The satin stitch completely encloses the raw edge, preventing raveling. It has a crisp, durable edge finish that in turn gives a well defined image. This is totally different from the softer edge obtained with Mock Hand appliqué techniques that use a turned-under edge.

Using two layers of fabric and a background stabilizer such as freezer paper (refer to page 21), stitch a few rows and adjust the width to about ⅛" wide. Adjust the length to feed evenly without either gaps

Obtaining a satin stitch length

between the stitches or jams from piling the stitches in too close. Do not use your hands on the fabric when making these adjustments; allow the feed dogs to do all the feeding.

The ridge of satin stitches should be wide enough to completely encase the raw edges of an applique piece. This will prevent raveling through many launderings. Each swing of the needle should catch approximately five to seven threads of the appliqué fabric. This is generally ⅛" wide or smaller. Try not to let the stitches get too wide, or the appliqué will have a bulky, heavy look.

After you have found width and length settings that you are happy with, the top and bottom tensions need to be adjusted. Start by loosening the top tension slightly. The buttonhole tension setting is a good place to start. Sew a line of stitches and look on the back side. If the tension has been adjusted adequately, there should be a bar of bobbin thread running down the center of the stitching on the wrong side of the fabric, or there might be color on one side only.

There should be no bobbin thread showing on the top side. If there is, you probably need to tighten the bobbin tension as well as loosen the top. If the top tension gets too loose, the stitch will loop. You want a tight stitch, where top thread color shows on the bottom but no bobbin thread shows on the top. This way, you do not have to constantly change the bobbin thread to a color that matches the top thread. It is more economical and a real timesaver!

NOTE: *These tension adjustments must be made to have the proper stitch whether you are using a left-, center-, or right-needle position.*

Satin Stitch Appliqué

1) *Christmas Goose.* Satin stitched wall quilt made by the author. Adapted from a discontinued pattern designed by Terry Thompson.

2) *His Nibbs and Matilda*
Extra fine satin stitch detail shows on these two charming folk art designs by Jo Sonja. Stitched by the author.

5) Critters Circus by Debora Konchinsky. Debora designed this quilt around the fabrics. Decorative stitches and specialty threads were added to satin stitch to achieve an exciting and fun effect.

4) Dogwoods. A bargello pattern was adapted to create this design. Satin stitching and blanket stitching were used for detail. The flowers are hand stenciled. Stitched by Estelle DeRidder.

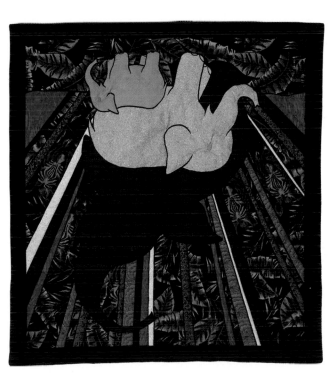

3) Saggy Baggy Elephants by Kathy Nicklas. Wall quilt was made for the 1989 Hoffman challenge. This is an original pattern designed by Kathy and totally satin stitched.

7)Folk Art Treeskirt
Designed and satin stitched by Kathy Nicklas. Kathy adapted patterns from Snowbound and American Country Christmas to create this piece.

6c) Example of Satin Stitch Appliqué

6d) Example of Mock Hand Appliqué

8) Twelve Days of Christmas. Pattern by Porcupine Hill Patterns. Satin stitched by the author. A lovely Christmas quilt inspired by a Christmas card using trims and machine embroidery for details.

9) *Detail of Drummer Boy From Twelve Days of Christmas*

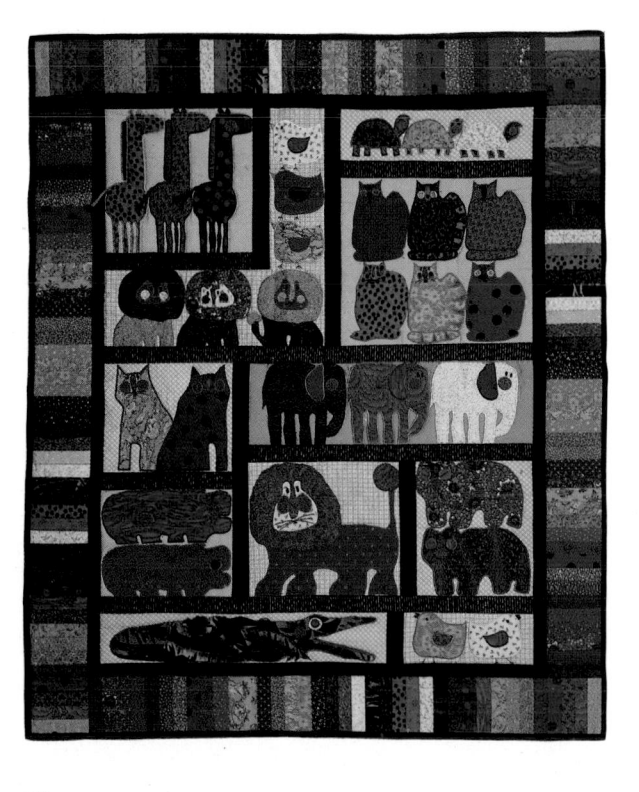

10) Rainbow Over My Zoo. Satin stitched by Kathy Nicklas. This delightful pattern by Anna Holland makes a colorful baby quilt.

Satin Stitch Appliqué

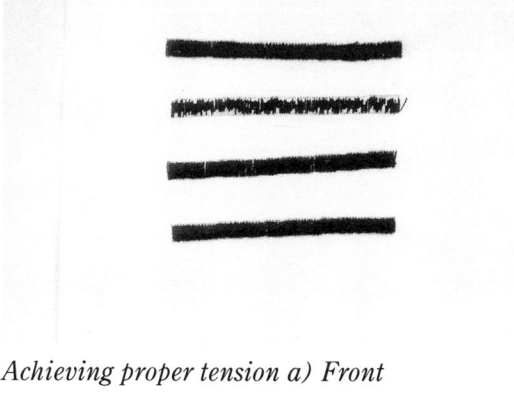

Achieving proper tension a) Front

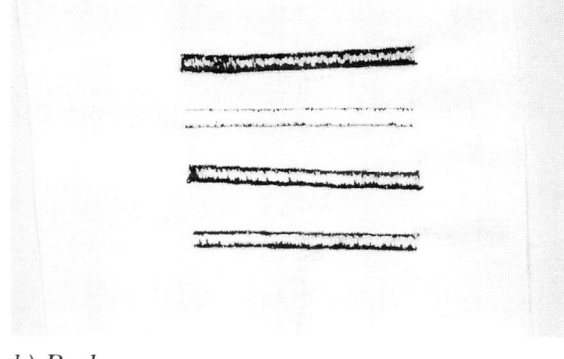

b) Back

Don't forget that you may need to readjust the tension for different sewing conditions. The weight and thickness of the fabric, number of layers, thread size and quality, spool size, and even how the thread is wound on the spool all affect the thread tension. Regularly check the back of your work as you sew to be sure that the threads remain properly balanced. (Refer to page 30 for detailed information on tension.)

Next, test different stabilizers. Even with the tensions adjusted and loosened on top, the heaviness of the satin stitching can pull the fabric inward between the needle swings, causing a tunneling effect in the fabric.

Tunneling

Tunneling can result in distortion of the background fabric and a puckered appliqué. Using a sturdy enough stabilizer will eliminate this. Generally, a heavy fabric needs a lightweight stabilizer, but a lighter-weight fabric needs a stiffer stabilizer. Practice satin stitching with different combinations until you feel comfortable with the products discussed on page 21 and the combinations needed to obtain flat, even stitches and appliqués. You will find that stitching without stabilizers not only creates tunneling, but the machine will not be able to feed the fabric evenly and will often stretch the fabric as it feeds. The stabilizer also affects the evenness of the stitches.

Next, you must learn to control the fabric with your left hand, while making width adjustments with your right hand.

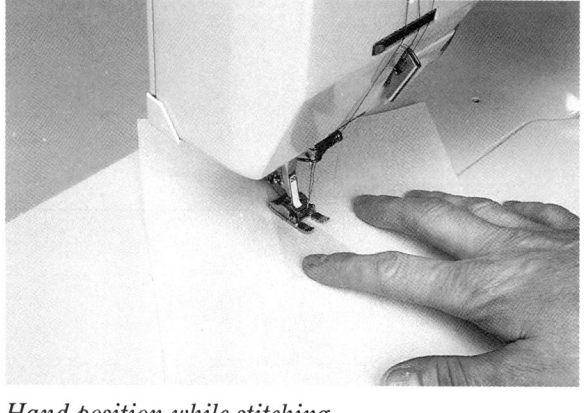

Hand position while stitching

While sewing a line of satin stitches, turn the width dial very slowly to a narrower then a wider width, going to the extreme each way. Then turn the dial quickly. The more slowly you make the adjustments, the more elongated the tapers will be. If the dial is adjusted quickly, the tapers are choppy. You will encounter points and angles requiring both types of adjustments, so get comfortable with changing the width as you sew.

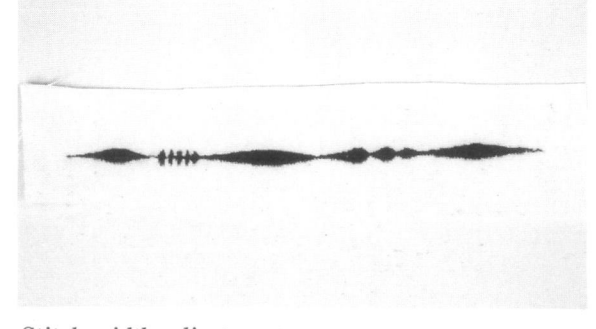

Stitch width adjustments

Now move the needle position to the right. Again, sew a line of stitches and adjust the width dial. The stitches will appear flat on the right side and will get wider to the left side. If the needle position is moved to the left, the left side of the stitches will be flat and will widen to the right. This is useful in achieving the look of mitered corners or for any number of decorative uses.

Effects of left and right needle position

TIP: *Check the stitch tension as you taper. Often the bobbin thread will appear on the top when you go into a very narrow stitch. Tighten the bobbin and loosen the top in very small increments until you have corrected the problem.*

Preparing your Samples

Now that your machine is set for satin stitching, the next step is to prepare the shapes on page 50 in fabric. Refer to Chapter Three for preparation techniques. Practice the stitching techniques explained below. These exercises will help you obtain perfect points (both inside and outside), corners, curves and miters. Practice these techniques on scraps of fabric, then move on to a design of your choosing. Soon you will be doing perfect satin stitching!

After you have the shapes cut out and fused onto a background fabric, place a piece of freezer paper behind the background fabric. Now, let's appliqué.

Locking off thread at beginning

As a rule, whenever possible, start stitching in the middle of a straight line or gentle curve. Try not to begin stitching at a point, corner, or curve. Pull the bobbin thread up to the top of the fabric by taking one stitch, making sure that the machine's thread take-up lever is at its highest position. Pull on the thread, and

the bobbin thread should come up through the needle hole. This allows you to hold both threads to eliminate any possible jams as you start stitching. Holding both threads, take several very small, straight stitches. This locks the thread in place. Cut the thread tails close to the surface of the fabric.

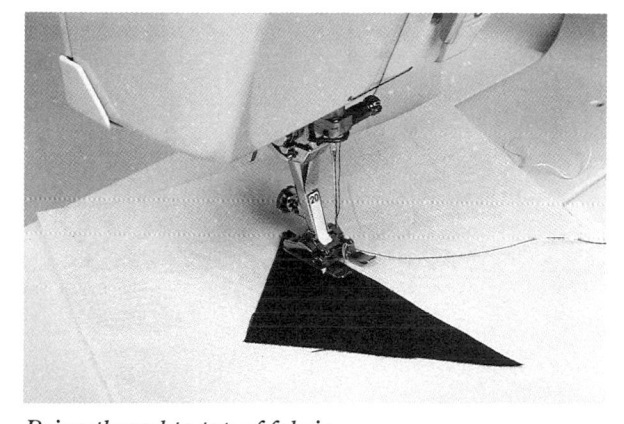

Bring thread to top of fabric

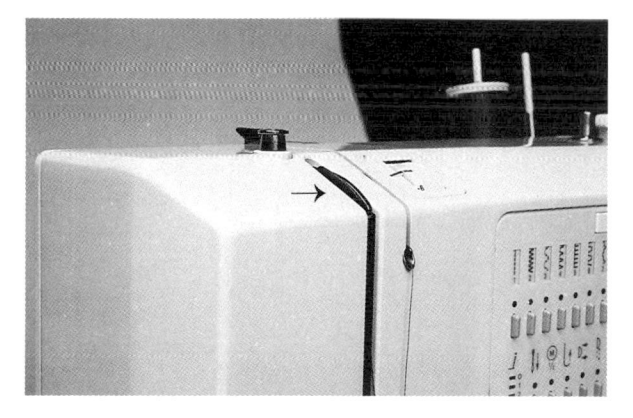

Thread take-up lever position

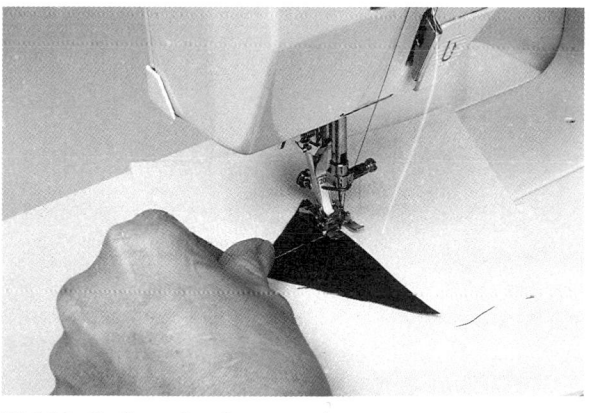

Hold both threads when starting

Straight Lines—Using bar shape #1

When satin stitching, the entire stitch width is on the appliqué. When the needle is in the right-hand swing or position, it should be just off the edge of the

appliqué. Train your eye to watch the needle as it swings to the right with each stitch, and keep the needle and appliqué edge aligned at all times. If the needle is too close to the edge, a frayed, hairy edge results. If the needle is too far from the edge, the edge will not be secured sufficiently and the satin stitch will not appear smooth.

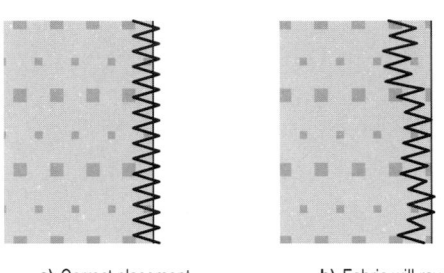

a) Correct placement   b) Fabric will ravel

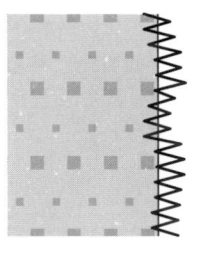

c) Fabric will pull out

Needle placement on edge of fabric

Practice positioning the needle on the edge by stitching down both sides of the bar shape you have prepared. Do not worry about turning the corners on this example.

Corners—Using "L" shape #2

Corners are the easiest elements of appliqué to maneuver. When you get to the corner, allow the right-hand swing of the needle to fall just off the appliqué edge into the background fabric, and just off the front edge of the appliqué. Do not stitch one stitch beyond the raw edges.

Inside Corner

Stitch to the raw edge at the bottom of the angle. Continue to stitch past this point until you have stitched into the body of the appliqué the width of the stitch (figure a). Stop the needle in the left-hand position. Pivot 90°. The needle should be aligned with the upcoming edge. The first stitch in the new direction should be made manually by taking one stitch with the hand wheel of your machine. This positions the needle in the right swing position. Move the fabric just a fraction so that the first stitch will be just barely inside and on top of the satin stitches. This prevents the first stitch from making a loop behind the first bar of satin stitching. The needle should also be aligned with the new raw edge to be stitched. Cross over the corner, and continue stitching down the raw edge (figure b).

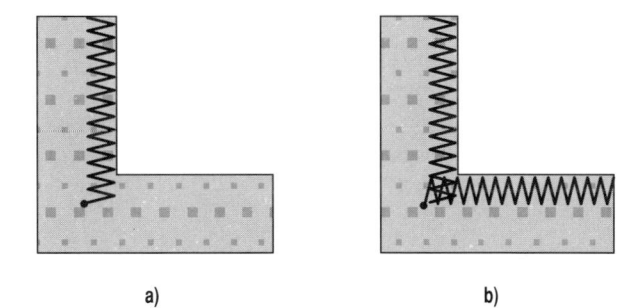

a)   b)

a) Stitch beyond cut corner as far as the stitch is wide   b) Pivot, reposition the needle and fabric

Outside "Crossover" Corner

Stitch until the appliqué piece is completely covered and the needle is just off the edge of the appliqué corner. Stop with the needle in the fabric in the right-hand swing, and pivot 90°. The next stitch will be made manually so that it will fall into the satin

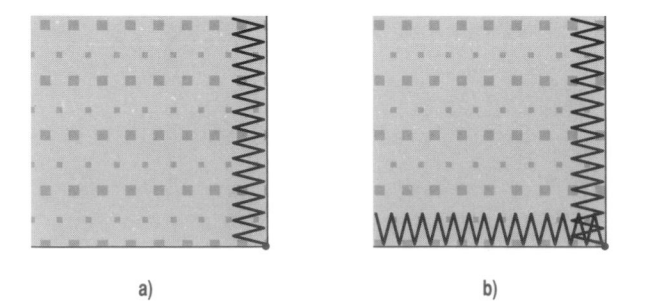

a)   b)

*a) Stitch to the edge of the fabric
b) Pivot, reposition the needle and fabric*

stitch instead of into the background fabric. Using the hand wheel, take a stitch so that the needle is in the left position, and position the fabric so that the needle is just barely in from the edge of the satin stitching. The first stitch is on the satin stitching. Continue stitching on top of the satin stitching, "crossing over" it.

Outside "Butted" Corner

This technique is used when you need the corners of two opposite sides to match. Stitch until the appliqué piece is completely covered and the needle is just off the edge of the fabric. Stop with the needle in the *left* swing and pivot 90°. Take the next stitch manually, turning the hand wheel until the needle is in the right swing. The needle is now aimed into the background fabric, not along the edge of the appliqué. Reposition the fabric so that the needle now goes into the hole that the top thread is coming out of. This allows the new line of satin stitching to "butt" up against the previously stitched edge, without crossing over. Instead of a stacked appearance, it gives the effect of stitching both sides of an end first, then the end itself.

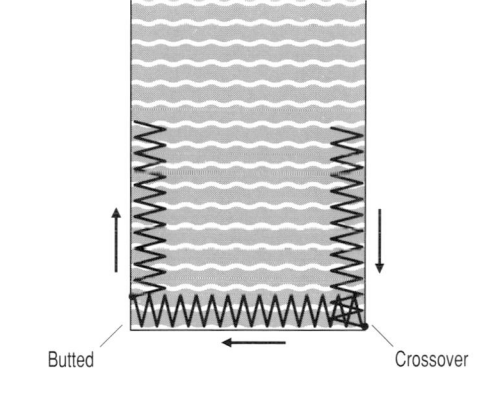

Butted   Crossover

Corner on right is crossed over, corner on left is butted to create the look of a bar across the end

Mitered Corner

If your machine has a right- and left-hand needle position, you can do a mitered corner. Stitch down the edge to the corner. At the corner, stop with the needle up and put the machine into the right-hand needle position mode. Turn the stitch width to "0". Lower the needle into the background fabric at the exact corner of the appliqué piece. Position your right hand on the stitch width lever. *Slowly* stitch while increasing the

stitch width. When you get to the edge of the satin stitching of the first side, you should be back to your original stitch width. With the foot down and the needle up, change the needle position mode back to center. This technique will take a bit of practice.

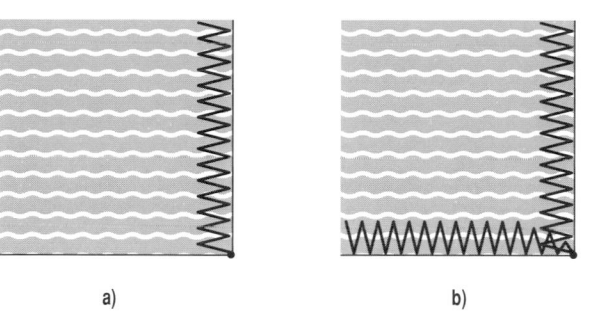

a)   b)

a) Stitch to the corner b) Turn width to "0" and gradually increase the width of stitches to achieve miter

Finish the last two corners with the technique of your choosing. Lock your stitches as explained on page 38.

Scalloped Corner—Using shape #3

Mark the middle of the scallop (a). Stitch until the needle hits this mark on its left-hand swing (b). Set the needle position mode to the left and the stitch width to "0". As you come to the raw edge, the stitch width should be back to normal width (c). Change the needle position mode back to center.

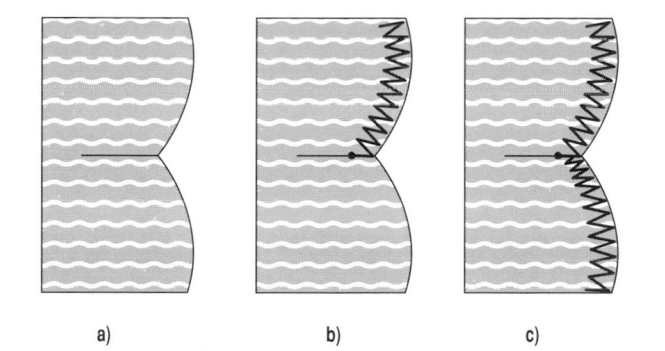

a)   b)   c)

a) Mark middle of scallop b) Stitch until needle hits mark c) Needle position on left and on "0" width, gradually increase to a wider stitch

Curves—Using shape #4

Pivoting is necessary when stitching around curved areas. It allows you to realign the edge of the appliqué with the needle as the fabric changes

direction. Without pivoting, slanted stitches appear, giving the edge a messy finish.

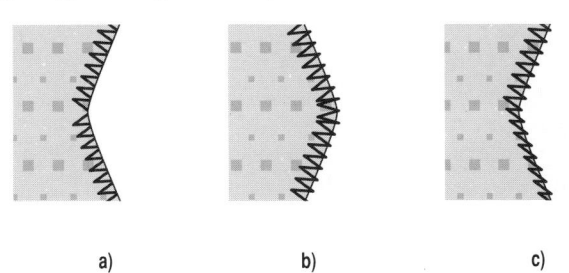

Problems resulting from improper pivoting:
a, b) Gaps from pivoting on the wrong side of the
needle's swing c) Slanted stitches from no pivoting

To change the direction of your stitching by pivoting, simply stop the machine with the needle in the fabric and raise the presser foot, then reposition the fabric. Only a very slight turn of the fabric is necessary. You will know when to pivot by finding that you cannot align the fabric fast enough while stitching to prevent slanted stitches.

TIP: The stitches should always be perpendicular (at right angles) to the cut edge, never at a slant.

Start with the outside curve of your ring shape.

Outside Curve

Pivot with the needle in its right-hand swing. On an outside curve, the needle is on the outside of the appliqué piece. A large or gentle curve will require only two or three pivots, and often, by running the machine at full speed, these slight curves can be done beautifully without pivoting at all. More frequent pivoting is necessary on tight curves. You might find it helpful to stitch a few stitches (counting them), then pivot

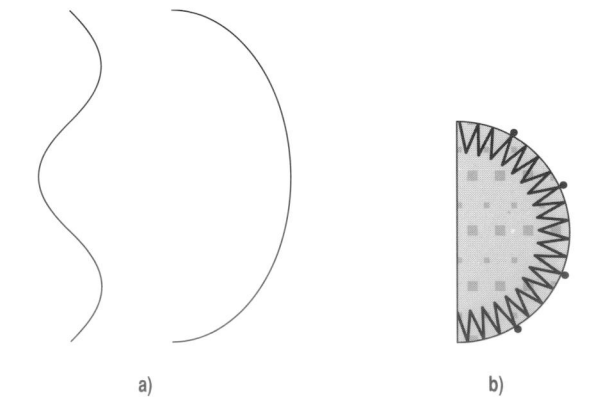

a) Gentle and large curves generally do not require
pivoting b) Dots signify that needle is on outside swing
when pivoting on an outside curve

slightly and stitch the same amount of stitches, and pivot again. Continue this until the ring circle is completed, and lock off the stitches.

Inside Curve

Pivot when the needle is on the left-hand side of the stitch. On an inside curve, the needle is on the inside of the appliqué piece. Inside curves are generally tighter curves than outside curves, so you will need to do more pivoting. Go slowly and count the stitches, as described above for outside curves. When through with the ring, lock off the stitches.

Dots signify that needle is on the
inside swing when pivoting on
an inside curve

Remember: Pivoting while the needle is on the wrong side of its swing leaves gaps in the row of stitching. Pivoting when the needle is on the correct side of its swing allows the thread to stack up slightly, creating a solid line of even stitches. No pivoting at all leaves slanted stitches that are unattractive and don't secure the raw edges properly.

Points—Using shape #5

Points can be tricky, and inside points almost elusive. But with practice these elements become fun and the showcase of your stitching skills. Start with the inside points.

Inside Points

When learning to stitch inside points, it is helpful to draw a line from the upcoming edge on the other side of the corner into the body of the appliqué for a guide. Eventually, you will be able to do this by eye, without the line (a).

Stitch the edge to the bottom of the "V" created by the point. Continue stitching into the fabric as deep as the width of the stitching used. You will be stitching straight until your needle hits the line you have drawn on its left-hand swing. Stop with the needle down in the left-hand position. Pivot until the foot is aimed

down the raw edge of the other side. The next needle swing will be to the right. It is now necessary to reposition the fabric before taking the next stitch. Lift the needle and move the fabric slightly to the right so that the needle goes back into the same hole that the thread is coming out of. Align the foot with the upcoming edge and continue stitching (b).

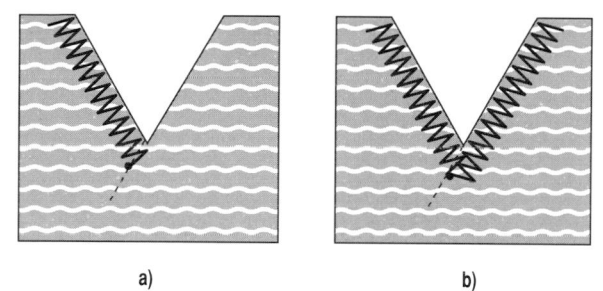

a) Draw placement line and stitch to line
b) Stop with needle on left, pivot, reposition fabric with needle swing

If the first row of stitching is not deep enough into the fabric, the stitches will not overlap and will give you two blunt ends of stitching (a). The cut point is not secured and the fabric is likely to fray and ravel after a few washings. If you stitch too deep into the fabric when you pivot, the stitching will cross over into an "X", leaving two ends out of alignment (b). Practice will correct both of these problems.

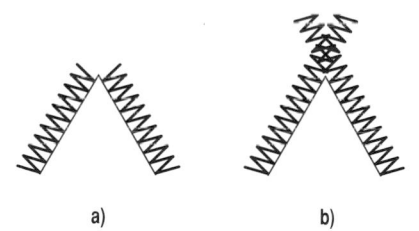

Problems resulting from inaccurate stitching:
a) Not stitching deep enough
b) Stitching beyond pivot point

Pointed Inside Points

With a washout marker, draw the shape that the satin stitch needs to make on the inside point (a). Once you have the guidelines drawn in, you can taper the stitches to give a pointed effect. Stitch until the needle hits the line marked on the right side. Pivot the fabric slightly so that the foot and point are aligned. Gradually reduce the width of the stitch to match the lines

drawn. At the end of the point, you should be at "0" width. Pivot. As you stitch up the next side of the point, gradually widen the stitch to normal, and pivot slightly to accommodate the angle of the edge.

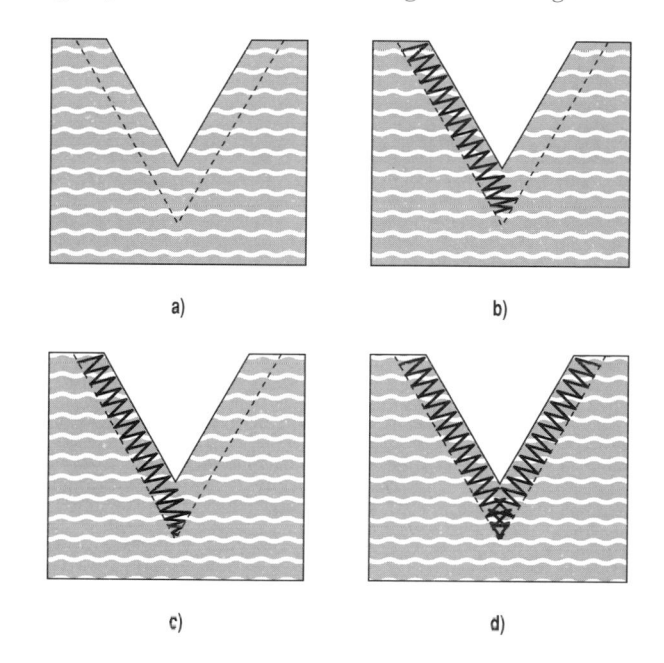

a) Draw in point shape
b) When needle swing reaches line, begin to taper
c) Taper to "0" width and pivot
d) Gradually increase to normal stitch width

Outside Points

These points are easy to understand, but they take a bit more practice to perfect. Stitch along the raw edge, keeping the width consistent until the needle is just beginning to stitch beyond the raw edge of the left side of the point. Pivot the fabric slightly to bring the point into the center of the foot. This will help prevent a curve from forming.

Gradually decrease the width of the stitch while you are sewing. Your guide here is to always have the needle rubbing both raw edges. The amount by which you decrease is dictated by the taper of the point. The stitch width should never be wider or narrower than the point. By the time you are at the very end, you should be at "0" width, and the point should be totally encased with stitches. Pivot.

Stitch out of the point by increasing the stitch width at the same rate that you decreased it. The width will increase as the width of the point increases. When you have returned to normal width and the needle is no longer on the left edge, pivot slightly with the needle

in the left swing and align the foot with the upcoming edge. Continue stitching. Finish the other two points and lock off the stitches.

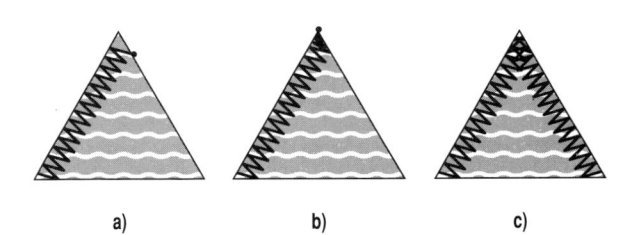

a) *Stitch until needle crosses to both raw edges*
b) *Taper so that needle stays on the raw edges*
c) *At point you are at "0" width. Pivot and gradually increase back to normal width*

Locking off threads at end of stitching

Once you have returned to where you started, or at the end of a piece, you must lock off the thread tails. If you are coming back around to where you started the stitching, as with the "L" shape, stitch two to three stitches on top of the first ones. Then change your needle position to the right, and put the stitch width to "0". Stitch several tiny, short stitches "in the ditch" of the satin stitch. They cannot be seen there and are very secure.

If you are stopping at the edge of another fabric, stitch three to four stitches into the next fabric and stop. Cut the threads. When you stitch the next fabric, the satin stitching will cover these end stitches and lock them in.

Checking for errors

After you have stitched your samples, look at them closely and compare your work to the samples

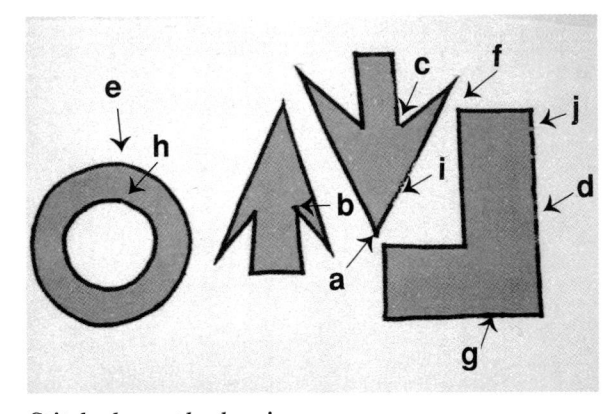

Stitched sample showing errors

below. Check to see if you have any of the problems indicated. Take the time to practice and correct any mistakes that you find before moving on to a project.

a) blunt point—stitch was not tapered
b) stitched too deep into point—"X" effect
c) not stitched deep enough—two blunt points
d) stitch length too long
e) gapped curve—pivoting from wrong side of needle swing
f) needle position not correct when turning corner
g) stitches piled up
h) gapped inside curve—pivoting from wrong side of needle swing
i) top tension too tight
j) skipped stitches

When mistakes are made on a project, correcting them by taking out the stitches is easier than you would imagine. Use a seam ripper and work from the wrong side. Cut through the bobbin thread only, and from the top, pull on the top thread. The stitches should unravel easily.

CHAPTER SIX

Building the Design

ow that you know the basic preparation and stitches, you are ready to try a design. After the appliqué pieces are cut out, they need to be put back together into the original design. Putting appliqués together is much like working a jigsaw puzzle.

Begin by laying the pieces out in order, and look closely at your choice of fabrics, textures, and colors. If there is anything that you want to change, do it now. Double-check to see if you have remembered to add the necessary underlapping extensions. Once you are satisfied with your choices, begin to build the design and secure the pieces to one another.

Appliqué Interfacing Technique

Using the original pattern and a light box, if possible, restructure the design. The pieces toward the back of the design will be covered by the pieces in the foreground, so begin at the back and work forward. Lay the original pattern on the light table, table surface, window, or any other surface that will help you see through fabric and paper.

Lay the most distant piece on top of the pattern. With a fabric-basting glue stick, start gluing the other elements onto that piece, using the pattern as a guide

Pattern on light box

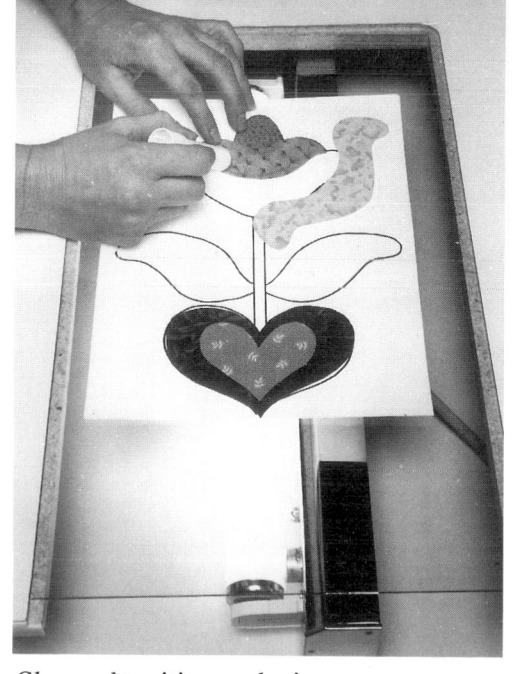

Glue and position each piece

for placement. (Do not glue the fabric pieces to the pattern—glue the extensions to the pieces that they attach to.) Once all the pattern pieces are in place, you should be able to lift the completed design and place it onto the background fabric in one piece. By building the design this way, you can center it perfectly onto the background fabric.

Again, check to be sure that there is nothing you care to change about your design. To change something, simply peel the piece off and exchange. The glue stick is water-soluble and will wash off without staining or leaving a residue.

When ready to secure the design to the background, apply glue stick to the very outside edges only. There is no need to completely cover the area with glue.

Press from back side

Fusible Web Technique

The fusible webs eliminate the need to work with the glue stick. However, once the pieces are ironed together, it is permanent, so be sure of the choices before building the design. You will again be working with the pressing sheet and the iron. Place your original pattern on the ironing board and cover it with the translucent pressing sheet.

Apply glue to edges of design

Place the design on the background fabric and rub gently to secure. Turn the background fabric over and press with a warm iron. This dehydrates the glue and prevents it from getting on the sewing machine needle in the stitching process, causing skipped stitches.

Pressing sheet covering pattern on ironing surface

Position design onto background fabric

Position pieces over pattern

Begin with the back pieces and start to place all the pieces of the design into position. Once the position of each piece is correct, gently set the iron on top of the fabric pieces. This allows the top piece to fuse to the extension below it. The pressing sheet keeps the the pieces from fusing to the pattern. Continue doing this until all pieces are placed and secured.

Lift design off pressing sheet

Press each piece in place

After the fabrics have cooled, gently lift them off the pressing sheet. Position the design on the background fabric, and press again with a hot iron, on both the front and back sides of the piece. The design is now fused to the background and is ready to stitch.

Place design onto fabric and press

CHAPTER SEVEN

Putting Theory Into Practice

The Love Tulip pattern presented here enhances your skills in maneuvering the fabric under the needle and introduces you to a design that consists of more than one shape or piece. You begin by building a scene and planning your approach to stitching order.

Select your fabrics, referring to the color photo of this cover, if you like. You will need fabrics of various shades: one color for each of the petals, the stem and leaves, and each heart. You will also need a 14" square of background fabric.

We will use the paper-backed fusible web technique for practice, as it is a readily available product and is quick to work with. You will need enough to trace the pattern onto. Then gather up machine embroidery threads to complement the fabrics you have chosen, and prepare your machine for satin stitching.

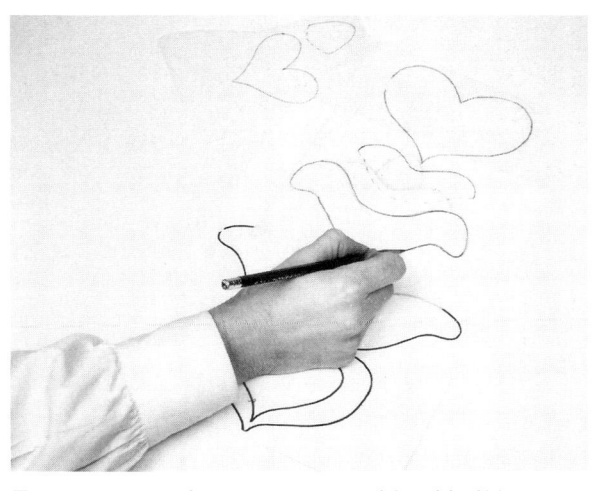

Trace pattern pieces onto paper side of fusible

Love Tulip—Step by Step

1) Trace the Love Tulip pattern found on page 51 onto a sheet of paper. Use a heavy black marker so that it will be easy to see when placing fabrics on top.

2) Identify the extension lines on the pattern and make sure you understand which piece they belong to. If necessary, retrace these lines with a red marker so that you will remember to add them to your tracings onto Wonder-Under.

3) Lay the Wonder-Under on top of the pattern, paper-side-up. Carefully trace the raw edge lines and the extension lines of each element of the design. This is a symmetrical pattern, so you will not need to trace anything in reverse image. You should have 8 pattern pieces when you are finished: 1 stem, 2 leaves, 1 bud, 2 petals, and 2 hearts.

4) Position each pattern unit of Wonder-Under onto the wrong side of each appropriate fabric. Press with a hot dry iron, following the instructions given with Wonder-Under.

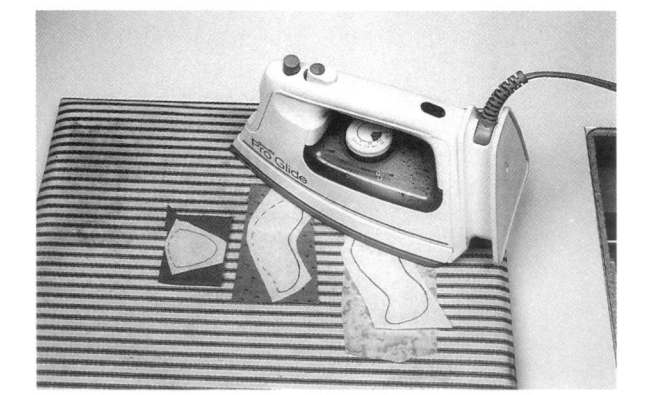

Pieces positioned onto wrong side of fabric

5) Cut out each pattern piece, being very careful and accurate when cutting the raw edges you will stitch. Remember: the smoother and more accurate your cutting, the cleaner your satin stitch will be.

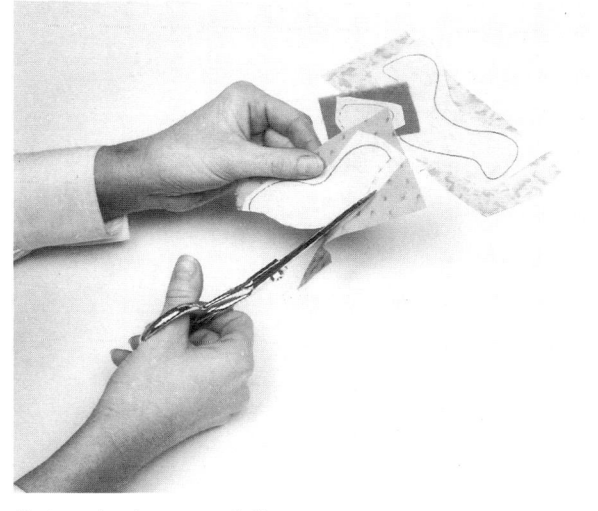

Cut each piece carefully

6) Lay the original pattern on an ironing surface. If you can see through the background fabric, place the fabric over the pattern and fuse the appliqué onto the background piece by piece.

Position background fabric over pattern on ironing surface

7) If you cannot see through the background fabric use this as an alternative method. Place the translucent pressing sheet on top of the pattern. This will allow you to fuse the pieces to each other first, then place onto the background. Carefully peel the paper backing off each piece, being very careful not to stretch or fray the edges. Begin positioning the units on the pressing sheet, using the pattern as a guide. Press the pieces to one another to avoid shifting. The pieces will stick slightly to the pressing sheet, making this easy.

8) Carefully lift the unit off the pressing sheet and position it onto the background fabric. Cover the

design with the pressing sheet to prevent the iron from distorting any edges, and press once again to fuse the entire unit onto the background.

Lift design off pressing sheet

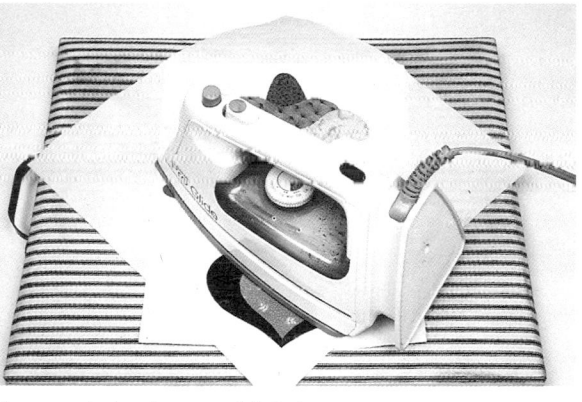

Press onto background fabric

9) Place a piece of your chosen background stabilizer (page 21) under the background fabric. Press in place if using freezer paper or Press and Tear; otherwise, pin in place.

10) Begin by stitching the leaves. They are underneath the stem, so they are the units furthest back. The ends of the leaves are sharp curves, so take special care to pivot enough to keep the satin stitch smooth.

11) The stem is next, because its ends are under the flower and heart.

12) Next, stitch the inner heart. Review the procedure for stitching inside and outside points on page 42. Continue by stitching the large heart.

13) Stitch the bud next, proceeding onto the first petal, then the largest petal.

You have now created a beautiful satin stitched appliqué. The more you practice these techniques, the cleaner and neater they get. Satin stitch is a lovely way to embellish many items, and it is durable enough to wear and wash.

The next half of this book, *Mock Hand Appliqué*, will introduce you to methods of appliqué that more resemble hand work. The Love Tulip pattern will be repeated with all of these methods. This way, you can get a feel for what look you prefer for different uses and projects.

The skills that you have learned with Satin Stitch will be of great help when continuing on with the Mock Hand techniques, which also require close stitching and manipulation of fabric edges. Be prepared for some exciting concepts in the next section. You will never approach appliqué the same way again! Have fun!

Practice Patterns

Love Tulip

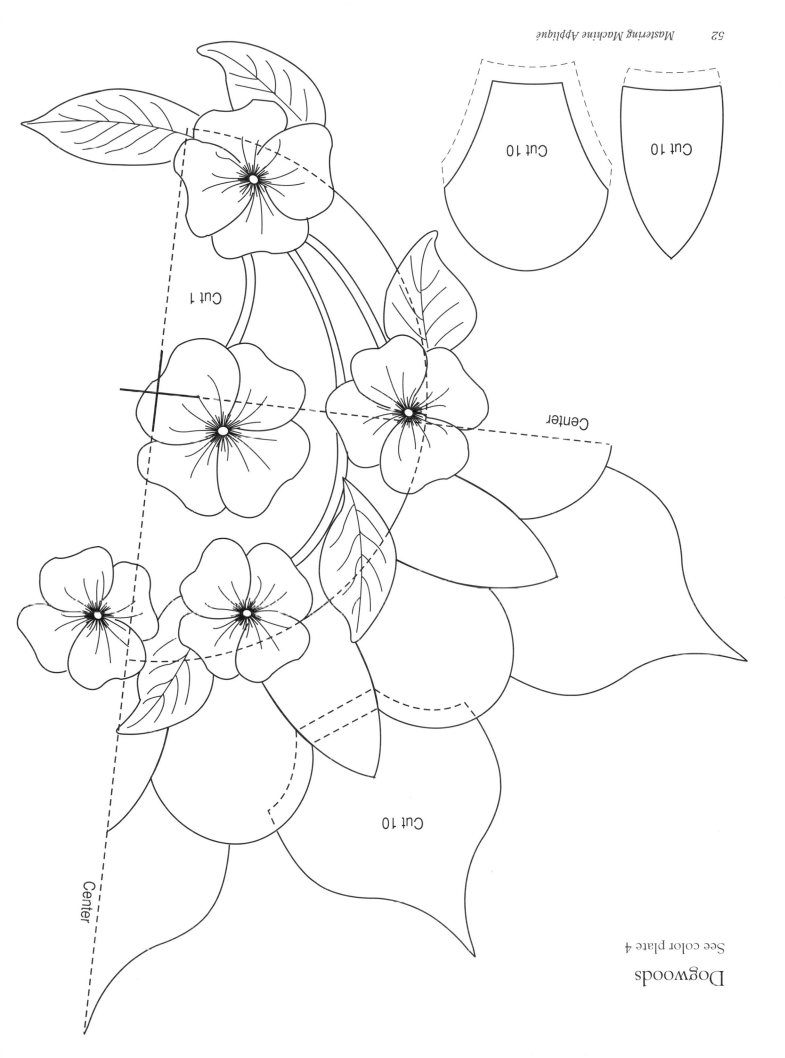

Cut 10

Cut 10

Cut 1

Center

Center

Cut 10

Dogwoods

See color plate 4